STUDIES IN LINGUISTICS

T0347418

Edited by
Laurence Horn
Yale University

A ROUTLEDGE SERIES

STUDIES IN LINGUISTICS

LAWRENCE HORN, *General Editor*

Negation and Licensing
of Negative Polarity Items
in Hindi Syntax

Rajesh Kumar

Routledge
New York & London

Published in 2006 by
Routledge
Taylor & Francis Group
711 Third Avenue
New York, NY 10017

Published in Great Britain by
Routledge
Taylor & Francis Group
2 Park Square
Milton Park, Abingdon
Oxfordshire OX14 4RN

First issued in paperback 2014

© 2006 by Taylor & Francis Group, LLC
Routledge is an imprint of Taylor & Francis Group, an informa business

Library of Congress Cataloging-in-Publication Data

Kumar, Rajesh, 1975-
 Negation and licensing of negative polarity items in Hindi syntax / by Rajesh Kumar.
  p. cm. -- (Studies in linguistics)
 Includes bibliographical references and index.
 ISBN 978-0-415-97646-6 (hbk)
 ISBN 978-1-138-01174-8 (pbk)
 1. Hindi language--Negatives. 2. Hindi language--Syntax. I. Title. II. Series: Studies in linguistics (New York, N.Y.)

PK1933.K86 2006
491.4'35--dc22   2005034354

informa

Taylor & Francis Group
is the Academic Division of Informa plc.

Visit the Taylor & Francis Web site at
http://www.taylorandfrancis.com

and the Routledge Web site at
http://www.routledge-ny.com

To Guddu

Contents

List of Abbreviations

AgroP	Agreement Object Phrase
AgrP	Agreement Phrase
AgrsP	Agreement Subject Phrase
AP	Adjectival Phrase
AspP	Aspect Phrase
Aux	Auxiliary
COMP	Complementizer
CP	Complementizer Phrase
DAT	Dative Case Marker
DO	Direct object
EMPH	Emphatic Marker
ERG	Ergative Case Marker
FEM	Feminine
FOC	Focus Marker
FUT	Future Tense
HAB	Habitual Aspect Marker
III	Third Person
IMP	Imperative
INF	Infinitive
INFL	Inflection
INTR	Intransitive
IO	Indirect Object
IP	Inflection Phrase

LF	Logical Form
MASC	Masculine
MOD	Modal
MoodP	Mood Phrase
Neg	Negation
NEG	Negation Marker
NegP	Negation Phrase
NP	Noun Phrase
NPI	Negative Polarity Item
PASS	Passive
PERF	Perfective Aspect Marker
PL	Plural Number
PP	Postpositional Phrase
PRESUM	Presumptive
PROG	Progressive Aspect Marker
PRS	Present Tense
PST	Past Tense
SG	Singular Number
SPC	Specificity Marker
Spec	Specifier
SUBJ	Subjunctive Mood
TP	Tense Phrase
TR	Transitive
VP	Verb Phrase
vP	Verb Phrase

Acknowledgments

Writing acknowledgements for any work marks its conclusion. Like every other graduate I have been waiting for this day. Now that the day is here, I am rather overwhelmed by the gap between how much I want to write and how little I am going to accomplish in a few pages. I came to the University of Illinois for my Ph.D. in Linguistics. I earned the degree and learned a lot more than just linguistics.

I would like first to thank the people who encouraged me and helped me make it all the way to Illinois. Among them, I must mention in particular Professor P.N. Jha of the Mithila University, Professor Rama Kant Agnihotri, and Professor K.V. Subbarao of the University of Delhi for their constant support and affection.

I am grateful to the members of my dissertation committee: Abbas Benmamoun, Rakesh Bhatt, Rajeshwari Pandharipande, and James Yoon. I wish to thank Professor Abbas Benmamoun, my dissertation adviser, for his guidance and support over the years. I learned a lot about linguistics from Abbas. My intellectual debt to Abbas is simply huge. I was really fortunate to have the opportunity to learn Syntax from Professor James Yoon. Together Abbas and James taught me how to conduct research in Linguistics (Syntax). I can never thank them enough. I am also thankful to Professor Rakesh Bhatt in many ways. He has always been there whenever I needed his help. His suggestions have always helped me in shaping up my work. I can confidently say he has been "a friend, philosopher and guide." Thanks are due to Professor Rajeshwari Pandharipande, who kindly agreed to be on my dissertation committee. From Hindi teaching to linguistics, I have learned a lot from her.

I am truly grateful to Rajesh Bhatt in the Department of Linguistics at the University of Massachusetts at Amherst. I have greatly benefited from his comments and suggestions.

Special thanks for their support are due to Professor Larry Horn of Yale University, editor of the Outstanding Dissertation Series at Routledge; Professor Patrick Olivelle, chair of Asian Studies at the University of Texas at Austin; Professor James Brow, director of the South Asia Institute at the University of Texas at Austin; and Sarah Green, associate director of the South Asia Institute at the University of Texas at Austin.

Max Novick, editor at Routledge, and Lauren Neefe at Stony Brook University deserve special mention. Where Max was very patient with a first-time author, Lauren extended her generous help in going through all the chapters and copyediting them. I am really thankful to both of them. Also I wish to acknowledge valuable help from Eleanor Chan of IBT Global, Robert Sims of Taylor & Francis Group, Himanshu Khurana and Urmila Patil of the University of Texas at Austin.

There are many other people I met during my stay at the University of Illinois at Urbana-Champaign to whom I am grateful. Any sort of attempt to thank my roommates and great friends Amit, Vaibhav, and Vijay would simply not work. They have been true support in every sense. They created the congenial and warm environment at home that was largely responsible for the successful completion of my graduate studies. They definitely did not help me in figuring out where negation is located in the clause structure of Hindi or how an element in Hindi is in the scope of negation or not, but the successful completion of my book does owe a lot to them in many ways. I survived the winter blizzards and summer humidity of the Midwest without any problems with the great warmth of their friendship.

Chapter One
Introduction

1. ABSTRACT

This study examines syntactic dependencies between negation markers and negative polarity items in Hindi. In order to do so, it first outlines a working clause structure of Hindi and locates negation markers within the clause structure. In Hindi clause structure, a negation marker heads its own maximal projection NegP, which is dominated by TP. In addition to locating the position of negation markers in the clause structure, this study outlines the distribution of negative polarity items in Hindi and the structural constraints on their licensing. I argue that the negative markers c-command the NPIs, and that this is a sufficient condition for the licensing of NPIs in Hindi. I also argue that NPIs are licensed overtly prior to scrambling. This work shows that the licensing of NPIs in Hindi does not involve any covert syntactic operations, such as LF movement or reconstruction. Finally, it shows that there are two different types of NPIs in Hindi, namely strong NPIs and weak NPIs. Strong NPIs require a clause mate c-commanding negative licensor, whereas weak NPIs are quantifiers and similar to the free choice 'any' in English, interpreted as NPIs in the presence of a c-commanding negative licensor. The data used in this study have been gathered from native speakers of Hindi.

There are two main aspects to the study of NPI licensing. The first aspect deals with how licensing principles are formulated and at which level of representation the licensing principles apply. The second aspect of the study of NPI licensing deals with whether the nature of licensing principles is purely syntactic (Jackendoff 1969, Lasnik 1975, Laka 1994, and Progovac 1994), and , purely semantic (Ladusaw 1979), or a combination of both syntax and semantics (Linebarger 1980, 1987). This study proposes a syntactic analysis of NPI licensing. The basic assumption in most of the studies on the licensing of NPIs (Lasnik 1972 and 1981, Laka 1989 and 1994, Mahajan 1990a, and Benmamoun 1997 and 2000) is that NPIs require a c-commanding negative licensor. In Hindi, a head final language, in which negative licensors occur at the immediately preverbal position, NPIs appear to occur higher in the structure than negative licensors. Thus, the negative marker does not c-command the NPI, and subsequently it fails to license it, under the assumption that the negative element must c-command the NPI. The questions that arise from this are as follows: (1) What are negative polarity items in Hindi? (2) How is negation structurally represented in Hindi? And (3) How are NPIs licensed? This study provides answers to these questions.

2. ORGANIZATION OF CHAPTERS

This study is organized as follows. The first chapter introduces the problem, summarizes various proposals, and briefly presents a summary of research in the field of negation and NPI licensing in English, Hindi, and other languages.

  The second chapter presents a detailed discussion of the clause structure of Hindi. A detailed study of Hindi clause structure helps to clarify the syntax of negation and the licensing of negative polarity items. In addition to discussing clause structure, this chapter focuses a great deal on the various characteristics of Hindi sentences. The first section of the second chapter presents a brief review of the typological features of Hindi, with particular reference to word order: the positioning of auxiliary verbs, ad-positions, complementizers, and modifiers. Then, it presents a detailed discussion of the various components of the Hindi sentence. It also discusses the structure of Hindi in the light of recent syntactic works and issues, particularly focusing on Chomsky (1989 and 1995) as discussed in Mahajan (1990a) and Kidwai (2002). Finally, I present a clause structure in this chapter that makes correct predictions with regard to the study of syntax of negation in Hindi. The proposed structure is not only a modification of existing proposals, but it is also consistent with the facts of Hindi, and dispenses with AgrP.

  In Chapter Three I present a description of the distribution of the markers of negation in Hindi. I also elaborate on the different positions of negation in clause structure, focusing on negation in different tenses, and imperative sentences, and, finally, on the interaction of negation with light verbs. It is the interaction of light verbs and negative markers that solves the puzzle of the categorical status and location of negatives in the Hindi clause structure. The second issue that I discuss in this chapter is the question of sentential and constituent negation. I present evidence in support of the immediately preverbal negation marker as sentential negation, argue that sentential negation is located outside VP, and suggest that negation markers head their own maximal projection and are located in a position dominated by TP in the clause structure of Hindi.

In Chapter Four I present a detailed discussion of the distribution and description of NPIs. I suggest that there are two types of NPIs, namely, strong NPIs (those that strictly require a clause mate c-commanding negative licensor) and weak NPIs (the elements that can be interpreted as NPIs both in the presence of a c-commanding negative licensor, and are also allowed in the questions, conditionals, modals, and adversative predicates). Later, I discuss the available accounts (Jackendoff 1969, Lasnik 1975, Ladusaw 1979, Linebarger 1980, Progovac 1994, and Laka 1994) of the licensing of NPIs in other languages, and, while doing so, I show the inadequacies of such analyses for giving an account of NPIs in languages such as Hindi. I also discuss the problems with an existing analysis for the licensing of NPIs in Hindi (Mahajan 1990a). Finally, I propose my own analysis, showing that NPIs in different positions are licensed overtly prior to scrambling. I show that NPIs are all licensed overtly and that the licensing of NPIs does not involve any covert syntactic operation.

In Chapter Five I discuss the nature of the two types of NPIs in Hindi: strong NPIs and weak NPIs. Strong NPIs are real NPIs, while weak NPIs are quantifiers that receive an NPI interpretation in the presence of a c-commanding negative licensor. There are systematic syntactic constraints governing differences between the two types of NPIs discussed here. Weak NPIs, such as *koi bhii* 'any' and *kisii bhii* 'any,' can be licensed by a long-distance licensor or by a negative licensor from outside syntactic islands. However, strong NPIs, such as *ek bhii* 'any,' *abhii tak* 'so far,' *kabhii* 'never,' *ek phuuTii kauRii* 'a red cent,' *Tas se mas na honaa* 'budge an inch,' and *baal na baaNkaa karnaa* 'to harm/ not being able to make a difference' specifically require a local licensor and cannot be licensed across syntactic islands. I show that strong NPI licensing in Hindi requires a c-commanding clause mate negative licensor. However, weak NPIs can be licensed long-distance in the presence of a c-commanding negative licensor. Weak NPIs do not obey locality restrictions such as island constraints (adjunct island and complex NP constraints). I further show that the basic assumptions of the existing analyses for the licensing of NPIs (Laka 1994 and Progovac 1994) are not required for the licensing of NPIs in Hindi. Finally, I suggest that weak NPIs are similar to the English free choice word 'any.'

3. THE PHENOMENON IN QUESTION AND
BACKGROUND LITERATURE

Some lexical items in natural language may require the presence of negation markers. Such elements are called Negative Polarity Items (NPIs). Some of the NPIs in Hindi are illustrated below in 1–6.

(1) a.   us   kamre meN ek   bhii   sTuDeNT nahiiN thaa
          that room   in   one   even   student   NEG   was
          * 'There wasn't any student in that room.'

     b. * us   kamre meN ek   bhii   sTuDeNT thaa
          that room   in   one   even   student   was
          * 'There was any student in that room.'

(2) a.   us   kamre meN koi   bhii   sTuDeNT nahiiN thaa
          that room   in   some   even   student   NEG   was
          * 'There was no/not even one (there wasn't any) student in that room.'

     b. * us   kamre meN koi   bhii sTuDeNT thaa
          that room   in   some   even student   was
          * 'There was any student in that room.'

(3) a.   raajiiv abhii tak   nahiiN aa-yaa
          rajiv   now   until NEG   come-PERF
          'Rajiv has not come so far.'

     b. * raajiiv abhii tak   aa-yaa
          rajiv   now   until   come-PERF
          * 'Rajiv has come so far.'

(4) a.   maiN tum ko ek   phuuTi kauRii nahiiN du-Ngaa
          I   you to one   broken penny   NEG   give-FUT
          'I will not give you a red cent.'

     b. * maiN tum ko ek   phuuTi kauRii du-Ngaa
          I   you to one   broken penny   give-FUT
          * 'I will give you a red cent.'

(5) a.   vo Tas   se mas nahiiN huaa
          he deviate   NEG   happen-PERF
          'He did not budge an inch.'

     b. * vo Tas   se mas huaa
          he deviate   happen-PERF
          * 'He did budge an inch.'

(6) a. raajiiv tumhaaraa baal baaNkaa nahiiN kar sak-egaa
    rajiv your   hair disturb NEG   do MOD-FUT
    'Rajiv cannot harm you.'

    b. * raajiiv tumhaaraa baal baaNkaa kar sak-egaa
    rajiv your   hair disturb do MOD-FUT
    * 'Rajiv can harm you.'

In the above examples the NPIs, such as *ek bhii* 'even one/any' in 1, *koi bhii* 'any' in 2, *abhii tak* 'so far' in 3, *ek phuuTii kauRii* 'a red cent' in 4, *Tas se mas na honaa* 'budge an inch' in 5, and *baal na baaNkaa karnaa* 'not being able to make a difference' in 6, are permitted in the (a) examples because they occur in the presence of the negative licensor *nahiiN*. The presence of a negative licensor is obligatory in all of the above examples, as shown by the ungrammaticality of all the (b) examples, where each sentence is ungrammatical in the absence of a negative licensor.

We find such elements in many languages. Let us consider some examples from English.

(7) a. There wasn't any student in that room.
    b. There was no/not even one (there wasn't any) student in that room.
    c. Rajiv has not come yet.
    d. I will not give you a red cent.
    e. He did not budge an inch.

(8) a. * There was any student in that room.
    b. * There was even one student in that room.
    c. * Rajiv has come yet.
    d. * I will give you a red cent.[1]
    e. * He did budge an inch.

In English, lexical items such as *any, even one, yet, a red cent,* and *budge an inch* are acceptable in the presence of a negative licensor, as shown in 7, but are not acceptable in the absence of a negative licensor, as the ungrammaticality of the sentences in 8 shows.

Much work has been done on this topic with reference to NPIs in various languages. In addition to the licensing conditions on NPIs, an issue that is closely associated with the questions of licensing conditions is the position of the negative licensor in the clause structure. Most studies assume the position of negation to be higher than the position of NPIs (Lasnik 1975, Linebarger 1980, Laka 1994, Progovac 1994, and Benmamoun 1997). This assumption is clearly seen through one of the commonly agreed-upon conditions on the licensing of NPIs: the negative licensor must c-command the NPI. In Chapter Two I discuss the position of the negative licensor in the clause structure of Hindi, and I suggest that negation in Hindi heads a maximal projection NegP and is dominated by TP in the clause structure.

The first study on negation within the framework of generative grammar can be found in Chomsky's *Syntactic Structures.* Chomsky (1957) derives a negative sentence from its underlying positive one. Klima (1964) later provides a detailed study of the syntax of negation in English. His study also discusses the derivation of negative polarity items from positive polarity items. Carden (1967) and Lakoff (1969) present semantic analyses of negation. Jackendoff (1969) presents an interpretive analysis of negation. In his analysis negation is generated in its surface structure (S-structure) position then climbs up the tree by interpretive rules, and thus takes wider scope. Lasnik (1972) discusses the scope of negation and its interaction with quantifiers and negative polarity items. His study assumes S-structure licensing of negative polarity items. Assuming the notions of command and precedence, he assigns a negative (+negated) value to quantifiers. Later, Horn (1989) offers the most comprehensive syntactic and semantic study of negation.

Linebarger (1980) clearly assumes that the licensing conditions on NPIs cannot be stated only in syntactic terms. She argues that the distribution of NPIs in English reflects an overlap of syntax and pragmatics. Her analysis of NPI licensing heavily relies on Baker (1970), who proposes that in the presence of an overt negation marker NPIs are licensed under the notion of c-command, and in the absence of an overt negation marker NPIs are licensed by implicature (pragmatic constraints). Linebarger's analysis also has two parts. The first part deals with cases of licensing in the presence of an overt negation marker, whereas the second part deals with cases of licensing of NPIs in the absence of an overt negation marker. For the first part she formulates a syntactic constraint, namely the "Immediate Scope Constraint (ISC)," which applies at LF. The ISC accounts for the following example:

(9)   He did not eat anything.

Linebarger's proposal involves two abstract assumptions: (a) some sort of LF operation and (b) some sort of abstract calculation of negative implicature. This proposal may have advantages over the surface structure account of NPI licensing by Jackendoff (1969) and Lasnik (1975) for languages like English. However, it may not carry over to languages such as Hindi. It is problematic for English as well. If the licensing of NPIs and scope of negation are determined at

LF, it is not clear what prohibits the occurrence of NPIs in the subject position in English. I discuss this in great detail in Chapter Four.

Ladusaw (1979), as a requirement for the licensing of NPIs, proposes that the NPIs be within the logical scope of the licensing elements, where the licensing elements are a subclass of "downward entailing" expressions. His is an attempt to reduce the licensing of NPIs to a purely semantic phenomenon, namely downward entailment, and it suggests that negation is one of the subclasses of downward entailing expressions. In this system an expression is downward entailing if it licenses inferences in its scope from superset to subset. The entailment is from superset to subset. Under the assumptions of the definition of downward entailment, Ladusaw proposes the following constraint: an NPI must be in the scope of a downward entailing element (such as negation), and if the downward entailing element is in the same clause as the NPI, the downward entailing element must precede the NPI. This constraint predicts the following acceptability judgment:

(10) a. Mary did not eat anything.
      b. * Mary ate anything.

This analysis also accounts for the acceptability of NPIs with conditional and universal quantifiers, as well as other contexts where NPIs are permitted, as in 11.

(11) a. If you have any pet, you will be allowed in.
      b. Everyone who has any pets will be allowed in.

Progovac's (1994) analysis of NPI licensing involves extending the analysis of anaphors and pronouns to polarity licensing. She claims that a Binding Theoretic analysis of NPI licensing accounts for the environments of NPI licensing shown in 12, where English NPIs seem to observe no locality requirements.

(12) a. John did not meet *anyone.*
      b. Mary did not say that John had met *anyone.*
      c. Did John meet *anyone?*
      d. If John met *anyone,* he will inform us.
      e. I doubt that John met *anyone.*
      f. John does not think that Mary said that she had met *anyone.*

Progovac suggests that NPIs are licensed under Binding Principle-A of the Binding Theory. For her, NPI licensing obeys the following universal and parameter:

"All NPIs must be bound and are subject to Binding Principles. Some NPIs are subject to Principle-A (English, Italian and Chinese NPIs) and some are subject to Principle-B (Serbian NPIs). Some NPIs rise at LF whereas others do not."

In the case of long-distance licensing of NPIs, Progovac allows NPIs to move at LF to be in the governing category of the negative licensor. Let us consider the following examples:

(13) a. Mary did not say that John had met *anyone*.
        LF representation:
     b. Mary did not say [$_{CP}$ anyone$_i$ [$_{C'}$ that [$_{IP}$ John had met t$_i$.]]]

     c. John does not think that Mary said that she had met *anyone*.
        LF representation:
     d. John does not think [$_{CP}$ anyone$_i$ [$_{C'}$ that [$_{IP}$ Mary said [$_{CP}$ t$_i$ [$_{C'}$ that [$_{IP}$ she had met t$_i$.]]]]]]

In 13 the NPI *anyone* is allowed to move higher at LF into the governing category of the negation marker *not*. The examples in (b) and (d) show the LF representations of (a) and (c).

Progovac's analysis is designed to account for the two types of NPIs in Serbo-Croatian. She calls them NI-NPIs and I-NPIs. NI-NPIs occur only in the presence of an overt clause mate negative licensor. If the negation marker is not within the same clause as the NPI, the sentence results in ungrammaticality. In other words, the NI-NPIs cannot have a long-distance licensor. Consider the following examples from Progovac (1994):

(14) a. milan   ne   vidi nista
        Milan   NEG   sees nothing
        'Milan cannot see anything.'

     b. * milan   vidi nista
          'Milan sees   nothing.'

     c. * milan   ne   tvrdi [da marija poznaje nikio-ga]
          Milan   NEG   sees that Mary   knows   none
          'Milan does not claim that Mary knows no one.'

In 14a the NPI and the negative licensor are in the same clause; hence the sentence is grammatical. In (b) there is no negative licensor in the sentence, whereas in (c) the negative licensor is in a higher clause. In both cases the sentences are ungrammatical, which shows that the NPIs and the negative licensors are required to be in the same clause for the sentence to be grammatical.

Though I-NPIs also require a negative licensor for their legitimate occurrence in a sentence, the negative licensor and the NPI cannot be in the same clause. If they are in the same clause, then the sentence is ungrammatical. In other words, the I-NPIs can only be licensed long-distance by a negative licensor in a higher clause. Consider the following examples from Progovac (1994):

(15) a. * milan ne zna ista
    Milan NEG knows anything
    'Milan does not know anything.'

b. milan ne tvrdi [da marija poznaje ko-ga]
    Milan NEG sees that Mary knows none
    'Milan does not claim that Mary knows no one.'

The sentence in 15a is ungrammatical, as the negative licensor and the I-NPI are both in the same clause. On the other hand, the example in (b) is grammatical, as the negative licensor is in the higher clause and the I-NPI is in the lower clause. Thus, the examples in 15 show, that the I-NPI and the negative licensor cannot be clause mates.

Progovac's (1994) approach to the licensing of NPIs is summarized as follows: along the lines of Generalized Binding of Aoun (1985, 1986), NPIs in Serbo-Croatian are anaphoric. To capture the distributional properties of Serbo-Croatian NI-NPIs and I-NPIs, Progovac suggests that NI-NPIs are subject to Principle-A and that I-NPIs are subject to both Principle-A and Principle-B . I-NPIs obey restrictions on Principle-B at surface structure but obey the requirements of Principle-A at LF. The negative licensor is not a clause mate of the I-NPI at surface structure, and I-NPIs move at LF to be bound within their governing category. Progovac (1994) thus demonstrates with various examples that the displacement of NPIs at LF to enable them to be in the governing category of a negation marker does not violate any conditions on displacement.

Progovac also discusses Serbo-Croatian NPIs in non-negative contexts and shows that only I-NPIs are allowed to be present in non-negative contexts, such as questions, conditionals, and adversative predicates. To account for the occurrence of I-NPIs in non-negative contexts, she proposes that there is a polarity operator in the Spec of CP in all such contexts, as shown in 16.

(16) a. $[_{CP}$ op $[_{C'}$ $[_{IP}$ . . . I-NPI . . .]
      b. $[_{CP}$ op $[_{C'}$ $[_{IP}$ I-NPI$_i$ $[_{IP}$ . . . t$_i$ . . .]

In 16 the governing category is the first maximal projection that contains INFL and the NPIs. I-NPIs are still not bound at LF. However, they can move at LF and be bound in the governing category, as stated above. In this case, the I-NPI is adjoined to IP (as shown in 16b), so that it is in the same governing category as its licensor in questions, conditionals, and adversative predicates.

Laka (1994) provides an analysis that assumes the presence of a negative CP. She differs from Progovac in that Progovac assumes that an operator in the CP is the licensor, whereas Laka assumes a negative CP is a licensor.

There are two reasons to propose such a hypothesis (Uribe-Echevarria 1994). First, it accounts for the occurrence of NPIs in sentential subjects, as shown in 17a below, where the NPI within the sentential subject is not c-commanded by the negative licensor. It also accounts for the occurrence of sentential objects, as in 17c below. Second, Laka's hypothesis provides an account of the asymmetry in the licensing of NPIs by a negative licensor and in the contexts of adversative predicates, as in 17e. The examples 17b, 17d, and 17f are LF representations of the examples in 17a, 17c, and 17e, respectively.

(17) a. That anyone might do anything like this never occurred to John.
      b. $[_{CP}$ [Neg] COMP [. . . I-NPI . . .]] $_i$ Neg V t$_i$

      c. John did not say that he saw anything.
      d. . . . aux Neg V $[_{CP}$ [Neg] COMP $[_{IP}$ . . . I-NPI . . .]]

      e. John denied that Mary ate anything.
      f. . . . V $[_{CP}$ [Neg] COMP $[_{IP}$ . . . I-NPI . . .]]

Evidence in support of the presence of a negated CP comes from the overt difference displayed by clausal complements in Basque. Sentential complements in negative clauses in Basque can appear with either–*e(la)* or–*(e)nik* suffixes. A sentential complement in a negative clause with the–*e(la)* suffix is interpreted to be out of the scope of the negative marker, whereas a sentential complement in a negative clause with the–*(e)nik* suffix is interpreted to be within the scope of negation. As the above-stated distinction predicts, NPIs are allowed only in sentential complements with–*(e)nik* suffixes. Consider the following examples:

(18) a. ez   dut uste [inor   etorri denik]
        NEG aux think anybody come aux-enik
        'I do not think that anybody came.'

   b. * ez   dut uste [inor   etorri denik]
         NEG aux think anybody come aux-enik
         'I do not think that anybody came.'

That an NPI is permitted only when the sentential complement contains the–*(e)nik* suffix is illustrated in 18. Because NPIs are licensed only within–*(e)nik* complements, Laka argues, this is evidence in favor of the presence of a negative COMP for the licensing of NPIs.

Having discussed the analyses mentioned above, I will now discuss Mahajan's (1990a) account for the licensing of NPIs in Hindi. Here he argues for an obligatory displacement of negation in Hindi at LF, offering upward LF movement of a negative licensor so that it will enter into a c-commanding relation with the NPI. Mahajan argues that the negative licensor moves higher at LF, adjoins to the finite IP, and licenses the NPI, as it does not c-command the NPI at S-structure. Consider the following sentences from Mahajan (1990a):

(19) a. koi   bhii t$_i$ nahiiN khaa-taa thaa sabzi$_i$
        someone even NEG   eat-HAB was vegetable
        'No one used to eat vegetable.'

   b. * koi   bhii t$_i$ nahiiN khaa-taa sabzi$_i$ thaa
         someone even NEG   eat-HAB vegetable was
         'No one used to eat vegetable.'

The example in 19a is grammatical, whereas the one in 19b is ungrammatical. Through these examples, Mahajan shows that the movement of the negative licensor at LF is obligatory. Once the movement takes place, the negative licensor is in a position from which it can c-command the NPI. In both (a) and (b) he provides evidence for such movement. According to Mahajan, 19b shows that the movement of Neg at LF is obligatory. The presence of the right-scrambled NP in the adjoined position, the AgrP, blocks the movement of Neg to the higher position. The presence of a right-adjoined scrambled phrase lower than the finite I in (b) introduces a barrier that blocks the negative licensor from moving at LF to a position where it can be governed by a finite I (Laka 1989). On the other hand, if the right-scrambled direct object is adjoined to the finite I (higher than the AgrP, as in 19a), then there is no barrier to block the Neg raising. Thus, in the cases where the Neg can move to adjoin to the IP, the Neg c-commands the NPI.

To account for NPI licensing, there is an alternative way to solve this asymmetry. Whereas in the first approach it is argued that the negative licensor moves at LF (Mahajan 1990a), in the second approach the NPI is argued to move lower, given the assumptions of reconstruction (Barss 1986 and Chomsky 1995, among others). In Chapter Four I present a critique of both these approaches to NPI licensing that involve covert displacement. I show how both approaches run into problems in providing an explanation for the licensing of NPIs in Hindi.

As we will see later in Chapter Four, the occurrence of NPIs in the subject position in Hindi poses a problem for most of the proposals mentioned in this section (Jackendoff 1969, Lasnik 1975, Ladusaw 1979, Linebarger 1980 and 1987, Laka 1994, Progovac 1994, and Haegeman 1995). Most of these analyses assume some sort of c-command, in the form of the command (Lasnik 1975), the assumption that NPIs are to the right of negative licensors (Jackendoff 1969), the Immediate Scope Constraint (Linebarger 1980), or the requirement that the NPI and the negative licensor be in the same governing category (Progovac 1994). None of these conditions on the licensing of NPIs provides a satisfactory account of the presence of NPIs in the subject position in Hindi.

In contrast to such analyses of NPI licensing, I propose that NPIs must be licensed overtly. The analysis that I present in this study shows that the licensing of NPIs does not involve any covert movement, either LF raising (Mahajan 1990a) or reconstruction (Chomsky 1995).

Chapter Two
Clause Structure of Hindi

1. INTRODUCTION

The aim of this chapter is to discuss the clause structure of Hindi. In addition to a discussion of the clause structure, this chapter will focus a great deal on the various characteristics of Hindi sentences. A detailed study of Hindi clause structure is important to the study of the syntax of negation and the licensing of negative polarity items in Hindi. This study helps to determine the location of negation in Hindi sentences and in the clause structure of Hindi. The location of negation clarifies and adds to the discussion of the licensing of polarity items.

In this chapter I first of all present a brief review of the typological features of Hindi, with particular reference to relevant items such as word order and the positioning of auxiliary verbs, ad-positions, complementizers, and modifiers. I then present a detailed discussion of the various components of a Hindi sentence. I also discuss the structure of Hindi in light of recent syntactic works and issues, particularly focusing on Chomsky (1989 and 1995), as discussed in Mahajan (1990a) and Kidwai (2002). I then discuss the clause structure presented in Mahajan (1990a and 1990b) and Kidwai (2002) and show how such proposals do not capture native-speaker intuitions regarding the syntax of negation in Hindi. Finally, I present a clause structure in this chapter that makes correct predictions with regard to the study of the syntax of negation. The proposed structure is not only a modification of existing proposals but also consistent with the empirical generalizations concerning Hindi, dispensing with AgrP.

2. TYPOLOGICAL FEATURES OF HINDI

Hindi, one of the most widely spoken languages of South Asia (India, Pakistan, and Bangladesh), belongs to the modern Indo-Aryan family of languages. In the following section I present a brief typological overview of Hindi.

2.1 Word Order

The basic word order of Hindi is subject-object-verb (SOV). As shown in 1a, Hindi is a verb-final (SOV) language, in which the verb is the final constituent of the sentence. The unmarked word order in a di-transitive sentence is SUB-IO-DO-V. The indirect object (IO) precedes the direct object (DO), as shown in 1b below (see Gambhir 1981, Subbarao 1984, and Mahajan 1990a for a detailed discussion of word order and related issues).

(1)   a. raajiiv   kavitaa   likh-egaa
          rajiv   poem   write-FUT
          'Rajiv will write a poem.'

      b. raajiiv-ne   sariitaa ko kapRe   di-ye
          rajiv-ERG   sarita   to cloths give-PERF
          'Rajiv gave cloths to Sarita.'

Unlike the word order of languages like English, the word order in Hindi is relatively free. SOV, however, does seem to be the canonical word order of Hindi. As a result of a rich agreement system (as discussed later in this chapter), Hindi allows various scrambling possibilities of constituents, resulting in various word orders. I provide a brief syntactic account of the scrambling operation (as discussed in Mahajan 1990b) in section 6 of this chapter. We will then see how this scrambling operation is relevant for the licensing of negative polarity items in Hindi. Consider the following sentences in Hindi. A simple sentence such as that in example 2 can have the various possible word orders shown below.

(2)   a. ravi-ne   sariitaa ko kapRe   di-ye
          ravi-ERG   sarita   to cloths give-PERF

      b. sariitaa ko ravi-ne   kapRe   di-ye
          sarita   to ravi-ERG   cloths give-PERF

      c. ravi-ne   kapRe   di-ye   di-ye   ko
          ravi-ERG   cloths   give-PERF   give-PERF   to

      d. kapRe   di-ye   ravi-ne   sariitaa ko
          cloths give.PERF   ravi-ERG   sarita   to

      e. kapRe   di-ye   sariitaa ko ravi-ne
          cloths give.PERF   sarita   to ravi-ERG

          'Ravi gave clothes to Sarita.'

The sentence in 2a shows the canonical word order of Hindi. In (b) the IO is left scrambled; in (c) the DO and the V (VP) are scrambled higher than the IO but lower than the subject. In (d) the VP (DO and V) are left scrambled higher than the subject; and in (e) the IO is left-scrambled, and the VP (DO and V) is scrambled higher than the left-scrambled IO.

2.2 Auxiliary Verbs

Hindi sentences can, in addition to main verbs, have auxiliary verbs. These are forms of the verb *honaa* 'be.' It is worth mentioning here that auxiliaries are marked only for present and past tense in Hindi. They also carry agreement information in both present and past tenses, but gender information appears in past tense alone. Auxiliaries follow the main verb in Hindi, as shown in 3.

(3) a. ravi   roz skuul jaa-taa   hai
          ravi-MASC daily school go-HAB-MASC is
          'Ravi goes to school every day.'

      b. sariitaa   roz skuul jaa-tii   thii
          sarita-FEM   daily school go-HAB-FEM was-SG-FEM
          'Sarita used to go to school every day.'

The sentence in 3a has an auxiliary verb, *hai* 'is,' in addition to the main verb, *jaanaa* 'to go.' The aux carries agreement features, namely Tense (Present in this case) and number (singular). On the other hand, the sentence in (b) has an aux, *thii* 'was'; it carries the agreement features of the Past Tense, singular number and feminine gender.

2.3 Ad-Positions

Hindi is a strictly postpositional language, as illustrated in 4a. It is never the case that we find an instance of a preposition in Hindi like that in 4b. Ad-positions in Hindi have various functions. Two of their major functions are case marking and specificity marking. Hindi does not have determiners such as the *a, an,* and *the* of English. The determiner *the* is a specificity marker in languages such as English, but in Hindi, postpositions such as *ko* are specificity markers (see Gambhir 1981 for details).

(4) a. ravi-ne   sariitaa ko kapRe di-ye
          ravi-ERG sarita   to cloths give-PERF
          'Ravi gave cloths to Sarita.'

b. * ravi-ne   ko sariitaa   kapRe di-ye
   ravi-ERG to sarita   cloths give-PERF
   'Ravi gave cloths to Sarita.'

In the above examples, the elements such as *ne* and *ko* are ad-positions. The ad-position *ne* is the ergative case marker, whereas *ko* can function as a specificity marker or as a dative case marker. In the example above, *ko* is used as a specificity marker and not as a dative case marker. I will present a discussion of the use of *ko* as a dative case marker later in this chapter.

2.4 Complementizers

The element *ki* 'that' is a complementizer in Hindi; it introduces embedded sentences and precedes them. This is illustrated in example 5 below. The main clause *raajiiv samajhtaa hai* precedes the complementizer *ki* 'that.' The clause following the complementizer is the complement of the main verb in the matrix clause. The complement clause may be either finite or non-finite. I discuss more about finite and non-finite complement clauses in section 6 of this chapter. The fact that the complement clause follows the verb in such cases is an unusual characteristic of word order in Hindi.

(5) a. raajiiv samajh-taa hai ki   us   ko   inDiaa jaana   caahiye
        rajiv   think-HAB   is   COMP him to   india   go-INF   should
        'Rajiv thinks that he should go to India.'

     b. raajiiv samajh-taa hai ki   vah acchaa kaam kar rahaa hai
        rajiv   think-PRES is   COMP he   good   work do   PROG   is
        'Rajiv thinks that he is doing good work.'

The sentence in 5a is an example of a non-finite complement clause, whereas the sentence in 5b is an example of a finite complement clause. As can be seen from the above examples, the complementizer *ki* 'that' in Hindi can precede both finite and non-finite clauses.

2.5 Summary

In this section I have briefly presented some of the distinctive typological features of Hindi. An appreciation of these features is important for a better understanding of the phrase structure of Hindi and of these features' structures, such as Case, Tense, and Aspect. It also helps establish a framework for the discussion of the syntax of negation and of the licensing of negative polarity items in Hindi.

In the following section I will look closely at sentences and discuss various components of the Hindi sentence. In addition, I will provide the internal structure of such components, namely the noun phrase, adjectival phrase, and verb phrase.

3. STRUCTURE OF PHRASES, CASE, TENSE, ASPECT, AND MOOD IN THE HINDI SENTENCE

This section presents a background for the structure of phrases and the feature structures of Case, Tense, Aspect, and Mood in Hindi sentences. As discussed previously, Hindi is an SOV language, in which the word order in a sentence with a di-transitive verb is S-IO-DO-V. In this section I discuss the different components of a sentence. A sentence basically has two main parts, namely the subject and the predicate. In addition to the subject, there are other main constituents, such as the direct object (DO), the indirect object, and the verb. In the following sentence, *raajiiv* is the subject, *film* is the object, and *dekh rahaa hai* is the verb-complex of the sentence:

(6) a. raajiiv   film   dekh rahaa   hai
        rajiv-MASC film   see   PROG-MASC   is
        'Rajiv is watching a movie.'

    b. sariitaa   film   dekh rahii   hai
        sarita-FEM film   see   PROG-FEM   is
        'Sarita is watching a movie.'

In the verb-complex in 6, *dekh* is the verb stem, *rahaa* is the Aspect marker (Progressive Aspect in this case), and *hai* is the auxiliary verb. Verbs carry Aspect, Tense, and Mood marking and carry Number, Person, and Gender agreement. In a Hindi sentence, Tense and Aspect markers modify the verb and the verb agrees with the subject in terms of Number, Person, and Gender. For example, the verb *dekhnaa* 'to see' is followed by the Progressive Aspect marker *rah* in 6a above, and the Present Tense marker *hai* in 6b. In addition to these modifiers, the verb agrees with the subjects *raajiiv* and *sariitaa*, respectively, and carries the masculine Gender marker *aa* and the feminine Gender marker *ii* on the respective Progressive Aspect markers.

In the following section I discuss the different types of phrases, such as the Noun phrase, Adjectival phrase, Postpositional phrase, Verb phrase, as well as their structures in the Hindi sentence. I will first of all consider the structure of a Noun phrase (NP), Postpositional phrase (PP), and Adjectival phrase (AP), keeping in view the head-complement relations within such phrases. I discuss the required functional projections that host such phrases in Hindi. The evidence shows that the head of a lexical projection appears to the right.

3.1 Noun Phrase (NP)

Noun phrases occur in the position of subject, indirect object, and direct object. A simple Noun phrase (NP) consists of a determiner or a quantifier and a noun (Bhatt 1999). Consider the following examples:

(7) a. *ek   laRkaa* aa   rahaa hai
        one boy   come   PROG   is
        'A boy is coming.'

     b. *koi   laRkaa* aa   rahaa hai
        some boy   come   PROG   is
        'Some boy is coming'

In the sentences mentioned above, *ek laRkaa* 'a boy' and *koi laRkaa* 'some boy' are Noun phrases. In 7a, *ek* is the determiner. A determiner can be numeral and pronominal. In 7b, *koi* is a quantifier, and *laRkaa* 'boy' is the noun. In some cases, as in 7c, an NP may take a sentential modifier.

(7) c. *raajiiv* jo dillii meN rah-taa   hai kal   aa   rahaa   hai
        rajiv who Delhi in   lives-HAB   is tomorrow   come   PROG   is
        'Rajiv who lives in Delhi is coming tomorrow.'

Specifiers, Genitives, and complements of nouns precede the noun in Hindi and are the head of the Noun phrase. The following examples in 8 illustrate this fact:

(8) a. yeh [laRkaa] meraa dost   hai
        this boy   my   friend is
        'This boy is my friend.'

     b. raajiiv kaa   [pitaa]
        rajiv   of   father
        'Rajiv's father'

     c. ek   bahut sundar [laRkii]
        one very   pretty girl
        'A very pretty girl'

The examples in 8 show the nouns in square braces; they also show that the Specifiers in (a) and (c) and the Genitive in (b) precede the noun. These examples illustrate that the internal structure of the Noun phrase is head final. In other words, the head of an NP appears to be to the right of the phrase, as in (b), where the Genitive *kaa* 'of' appears to the left of the head.

3.1.1 Modifiers

Modifiers, such as adjectives and relative clauses, precede the noun in Hindi.[1] In the following sentence, the adjective *ganda* precedes the noun *paanii*:

(9) gandaa paanii
     dirty   water
     'Dirty   water'

On the other hand, adjectives can also appear to follow nouns when the adjective occurs in a sentence as part of a predicate. It is important to mention here that a predicative adjective occurs in the preverbal position. In the following sentence, the adjective *kaalii* modifies the noun *kamiiz* 'shirt' and occurs as a predicate. Also it is in a preverbal position with respect to the verb *hai* 'be' in Hindi.

(10) merii kamiiz   kaalii hai
      my   shirt   black   is
      'My shirt is black.'

3.2 Postpositional Phrase (PP)

The complement-head ordering within a Postpositional phrase is consistent with the head final characteristics of Hindi. The head of a Postpositional phrase (a postposition) always occurs to the right of its complement and occupies phrase final position (Bhatt 1999). The following examples illustrate these facts:

(11) a. mere [ghar meN]   paaNc   kamre haiN
         my   house in   five   rooms are
         'There are five rooms in my house.'

      b. * mere [meN   ghar]   paaNc   kamre haiN
           my   in   house   five   rooms are
           'There are five rooms in my house.'

The example in 11a shows the Postpositional phrase in square braces, where the postposition *meN* 'in' follows the noun *ghar* 'house.' The occurrence of the head of a Postpositional phrase to the left of the complement results in ungrammaticality, as shown in 11b.

3.3 Adjectival Phrase (AP)

I will briefly mention the internal structure of an Adjectival phrase here. A discussion of Adjectival phrases is important, as some of the so-called NPIs, or, according to my claim, negative quantifiers, occur as adjectives to the nouns they have scope over. As mentioned above, adjectives precede the nouns they modify in Hindi, as well as occur in the predicate position. Now I will talk about predicative adjectives and argue that the head of the Adjectival phrase occurs to the right of the complement of the phrase.

(12) a. gaaRii calne ke liye taiyaar hai
      train walk for ready is
      'The train is ready to leave.'

   b. kamiiz kaalii hai
      shirt black is
      'The shirt is black.'

   c. * taiyaar gaaRii calne ke liye hai
      ready train walk for is
      'The train is ready to leave.'

In 12a and 12b, the adjective that is the head of the Adjectival phrase occurs to the right of its complement. In 12c, the ungrammaticality of the example shows that the structure of the Adjectival phrase is also head final (Bhatt 1999).

3.4 Verb Phrase (VP)

A Verb phrase contains a verb and its arguments and adjectives. In this section I will discuss the nature of verbs in Hindi according to the following: Case, Tense, Aspect, and Mood. A detailed discussion of case, tense, aspect, and mood in general and of their order in particular helps to determine the inflectional layer of the clause structure of Hindi. This discussion, along with a discussion of VP, helps in locating negation in the clause structure and in understanding the syntax of negation in Hindi. In Chapter Two I discuss the syntax of negation in Hindi, which has implications for the licensing of negative polarity items.

The facts regarding VP projection are similar to those regarding NPs and PPs in Hindi. In other words, the structure of the VP is also head-final. The verb occurs to the right of its complements and assigns them theta roles; it also assigns case to the argument to its left. Consider the following examples:

(13) a. maiN   kahaaniyaaN   paRh-taa   huuN
     I   stories   read-HAB   am
     'I read stories.'

   b. */? maiN   paRh-taa   kahaaniyaaN   huuN
      I   read-HAB   stories   am
      'I read stories.'

We see that in 13a the verb occurs to the right of its complements. When the verb precedes its complements, as shown in 13b, the sentence is awkward. [2] The head final fact of the Hindi verb phrase and the assumptions of the VP internal subject hypothesis lead us to a uniform mechanism of theta role assignment: all theta roles are assigned to the left by the verb to all its arguments within the VP.

3.4.1 Case in Hindi

In this section I will discuss the different cases in Hindi, such as Nominative, Accusative, Dative, and Ergative. Dative, Ergative, and sometimes Accusative Cases are marked by a postposition (see the discussion below, as well as Bhatt 1994 and 1999).

3.4.1.1 Nominative Case

Subject NPs in Hindi are marked with Nominative Case.[3] In other words, nominative case NP controls agreement with the verb. Although it does have markers for other Cases, Hindi does not have a marker for the Nominative. Look at the following example:

(14)   raajiiv   kahaaniyaaN   paRh-egaa
     rajiv-MASC-SG   stories-FEM-PL   read-FUT-MASC-SG
     'Rajiv will read stories.'

In 14 there are two NPs, namely *raajiiv* and *kahaaniyaaN* 'stories.' The NP *raajiiv* controls agreement with the verb from the subject position, as it is a singular and masculine noun and the verb shows singular and masculine inflection. It is also clear that the other noun, *kahaaniyaaN* 'stories,' being a feminine plural noun, does not control agreement. Thus, the NP *raajiiv* is in the Nominative Case. Later I will present a discussion of how NPs are assigned Nominative Case.

3.4.1.2 Accusative Case and Specificity

Now I turn to a discussion of Accusative Case in Hindi. Most of the time NPs with Accusative Case markers do not carry any marker, as in 14, above. The NP *kahaaniyaaN* 'stories' is the direct object of the verb *paRhnaa* 'to read' and is marked Accusative Case without any overt Case marker. However, in some cases we do see a marker, *ko*, functioning as an Accusative Case maker. It is important to mention that the overt Case marker on the object (particularly in the case of the direct object) is a specificity marker. As discussed previously in this chapter, Hindi does not have a determiner system like English (*a, an,* and *the*). In the absence of such a system, postpositions, such as *ko*, function as specificity markers, as in 15a and 15b.

(15) a. raajiiv   juute   ko   saaf   kar   rahaa   hai
         rajiv   shoes   SPC   clean   do   PROG   is
         'Rajiv is cleaning the shoes.'

      b. raajiiv   juute   saaf   kar-taa   hai
         rajiv   shoes   clean   do-HAB   do-HAB
         'Rajiv cleans shoes.'

In 15a, *juute* 'shoes' is specific, whereas in 15b it is not. In both cases, however, *juute* 'shoes' appears as the direct object. Since NPs followed by postpositions (in this case *ko*)[4] do not control agreement, it appears to be the case that specificity markers on the direct objects are Case markers. The difference between Nominative and Accusative Case lies in the ability to control agreement. In other words, only NPs in the Nominative Case control agreement; NPs in the Accusative Case never do.[5] The NP that controls agreement bears Nominative Case, whereas the NP that does not control agreement bears Accusative Case (Bhatt 1994 and 1999).

3.4.1.3 Ergative Case

We find Ergative Case in many languages of the world (Dixon 1994).[6] Hindi is one such language. In its (i.e., Hindi's) Ergative Case, the subject of a sentence is followed by an overt case marker *ne* and subsequently does not control agreement.[7] In this case, the object- present controls agreement. Interestingly, we find ergativity in Hindi in a very restricted environment. We find Ergative Case with the subject in Hindi only when the verb is transitive and it is in the Perfect Aspect. Later in this chapter, I discuss Perfect Aspect in detail. Because Ergative Case on subjects is restricted to transitive verbs and the perfect aspect, this division is called split ergativity[8]. For example, in the following sentence, 16, the subject *raajiiv* does not agree with the verb, as *raajiiv* is masculine, and the verb *likhii* 'wrote' has feminine agreement morphology. Hence, the verb agrees with the object, *kaviitaa* 'poem,' which is feminine. The subject also gets Ergative Case.

(16) raajiiv-ne   ek   kaviitaa   likh-ii
      rajive-ERG-MASC   one   poem-FEM   write-PERF-IIISG-FEM
      'Rajive wrote a poem.'

Since the transitive or intransitive nature of the verb is crucial for ergative case, I will briefly discuss it here. Verbs are mainly divided into two types: transitive and intransitive. There is yet another type of verb, that is, di-transitive. The intransitive verb takes no essential argument, the transitive verb takes one essential argument, and the di-transitive verb takes two arguments. The following examples illustrate this fact:

(17) a.   raajiiv   so   rahaa   hai
           rajiv   sleep (INTR)   PROG   is
           'Rajiv is sleeping.'

      b.   raajiiv   aam   khaa   rahaa   hai
           rajiv   mango eat (TR) PROG   is
           'Rajiv is eating a mango.'

      c.   raajiiv   sariitaa   ko   hindii   paRaa   rahaa   hai
           rajiv   sarita   to (IO)   Hindi (DO)   teach   PROG   is
           'Rajiv is teaching Sarita Hindi.'

The verb *sonaa* 'sleep' in 17a is intransitive, as it does not have any essential argument in the VP. The verb *khaanaa* 'eat' in 17b is an example of a transitive verb, and it has one argument in the VP, the direct object, *aam* 'mango.' The verb *paRaanaa* 'teach' in 17c is a di-transitive verb, as it has two arguments in the VP, the indirect object, *sariitaa ko* 'to Sarita,' and the direct object, *hindii* 'Hindi.' The other crucial part of the Ergative Case is Perfective Aspect, which I discuss later in this chapter, in section 3.4.3.3.

3.4.1.4 Dative Case

We find Dative Case on subjects only. In Hindi it is found in the context of some special predicates. These predicates are commonly known as "psych" predicates. The marker of Dative Case is the morpheme (or postposition) *ko*. The postposition or Dative Case marker *ko* never appears with direct or indirect objects. As I mentioned earlier, the marker *ko* with direct and indirect objects is a specificity marker. It is also important to mention here that psych predicates denote mental states. Consider the following examples:

(18) a. sariitaa-ko   gussaa   aa-yaa
        sarita-FEM-DAT   anger-MASC   come-PERF-MASC
        'Sarita got mad.'
        Lit: 'Anger came to Sarita.'

   b. raajiiv-ko   hansii   aa-yii
        rajiv-MASC-DAT   laughter-FEM   come-PERF-FEM
        'Rajiv started laughing.'
        Lit: 'Laughter came to Rajiv.'

   c. mujh-ko   aam   pasand   hai
        I-DAT   mango   pleasing   is.
        'I like mango.'
        Lit: 'Mango is pleasing to me.'

In the examples above, we observe that the Dative Case marker *ko* follows the subjects *sariitaa, raajiiv,* and *mujh*.[9] We also observe in these examples that the objects *gussaa* 'anger,' *hansii* 'laughter,' and *aam* 'mango' agree with the verbs in their respective sentences. Verbs such as *gussaa aanaa* 'to be angry,' *hansii aanaa* 'to feel like laughing,' and *pasand honaa* 'to like' are psych predicates in Hindi. I will discuss the distribution of NPIs in the context of dative subjects in Chapter Four.

3.4.2 The Tense System of Hindi

Hindi makes a three-way distinction with respect to Tense. In this section I present the distribution of three tenses, namely Present, Past, and Future. It is interesting to see that Present and Past Tense markers appear on the auxiliary verb, whereas the Future Tense marker appears as a morpheme on the main verb. This is the reason that the verb honaa 'to be' does not have a Future Tense form.

3.4.2.1 Present Tense

Let us consider the following example of Present Tense for discussion:

(19) raajiiv   DaakTar   hai
        rajiv   doctor   is/PRS
        'Rajiv is a doctor.'

The sentence in 19 is an example of Present Tense. The Present Tense marker is the auxiliary verb *hai* 'is' (Gambhir 1981, Guru 1952, Kellogg 1938, and Kachru 1965 and 1966). The Present Tense marker *hai* 'is' is one of the forms of the verb *honaa* 'to be.' The verb *honaa* 'to be' has different forms in the two different number distinctions (singular and plural). The Present Tense marker *hai* 'is' in 20a is singular, and the marker *haiN* 'are' in 20b is plural.[10] It is important to note here that the Present Tense marker does not inflect for Gender. In other words, the two forms are the same in (two) different genders, unlike their Past Tense counterpart.

(20) a. raajiiv   klaas   meN   hai
          rajiv   class   in   is
          'Rajiv is in the class.'

      b. raajiiv   aur   sariitaa klaas   meN haiN
          rajiv   and   sarita   class   in   are
          'Rajiv and Sarita are in the class.'

3.4.2.2 Past Tense

Let us consider the following example of the Past Tense. The Past Tense marker is another auxiliary verb, *thaa* 'was,' also one of the forms of the verb *honaa* 'to be' (Gambhir 1981, Guru 1952, Kellogg 1938, and Kachru 1965 and 1966).

(21) ek   gaaoN   meN   ek   raajaa   thaa
      one   village in   one   king   was/PST
      'There was a king in a village.'

These forms of the verb *honaa* 'to be' inflect for Number and Gender. With respect to inflection on the Past Tense marker for Gender, it is different from the Present Tense marker, as the Present Tense marker does not carry Gender information. For example, in the case of the Past Tense marker, *thaa* 'was,' as in 22a, is masculine singular; *the* 'were,' as in 22b, is masculine plural; *thii* 'was,' as in 22c, is feminine singular,;and *thiiN* 'were,' as in 22d, is feminine plural.

(22) a. raajiiv   ghar   meN   thaa
          rajiv-MASC-SG   house   in   was-MASC-SG
          'Rajiv was at home.'

      b. raajiiv   aur sariitaa   ghar   meN   the
          rajiv-MASC   and sarita-FEM   house   in   were-MASC-PL
          'Rajiv and Sarita were at home.'

c. sariitaa   ghar   meN thii
   sarita-FEM-SG house in   was-FEM-SG
   'Sarita was at home.'

d. siimaa   aur   sariitaa   ghar meN thiiN
   sima-FEM and   sarita-FEM house in   were-FEM-PL
   'Sima and Sarita were at home.'

e. sariitaa   ghar   meN hai
   sarita-FEM house in   is
   'Sarita is at home.'

f. raajiiv   ghar   meN hai
   sarita-MASC house in   is
   'Rajiv is at home.'

The examples in 22e and 22f show the contrast where the Present Tense markers do not carry any gender agreement.

3.4.2.3 Future Tense

The Future Tense marker in Hindi is not an auxiliary verb, unlike the Present and Past Tense markers. The Future Tense marker–*g* is a clitic on the verb. This clitic carries or hosts Number and Gender clitics. The Tense clitic precedes the Number and Gender marker morphemes (Gambhir 1981, Guru 1952, Kellogg 1938, and Kachru 1965 and 1966). The following examples illustrate these facts:

(23) a. raajiiv hindustaan jaa-ye-gaa
     rajiv   rajiv   go-FUT
     'Rajiv will go to India.'

   b. sariitaa hindustaan jaa-ye-gii
     rajiv   India   go-FUT
     'Sarita will go to India.'

In the example in 23a, the future tense marker clitic *ye-gaa* is carrying masculine gender, whereas the Future Tense marker *ye-gii* in 23b is carrying feminine gender.

3.4.3 Aspect

There are three Aspects in Hindi. They are the Habitual, Progressive, and Perfect. In this section I discuss the distribution of all three Aspects.

    The Habitual and the Perfect Aspect markers are clitics on the verb, whereas the Progressive Aspect marker is an independent lexical item. These

Aspect markers are inflected for Gender and Person (Gambhir 1981, Guru 1952, Kellogg 1938, and Kachru 1965 and 1966). The following sections further illustrate the three Hindi aspectual markers.

3.4.3.1 Habitual Aspect

The Habitual Aspect marker is–*t* in Hindi. As mentioned above, it carries Number and Gender information (Gambhir 1981, Guru 1952, Kellogg 1938, and Kachru 1965 and 1966). This is shown in the examples in 24 and 25 below.

(24) a. raajiiv   ciTThii   likh-taa   hai
     rajiiv-MASC   letter   write-HAB-MASC   is
     'Rajiv writes a letter.'

    b. sariitaa   ciTThii   likh-tii   hai
      sarita-FEM   letter   write-HAB-FEM   is
      'Sarita writes a letter.'

(25) a. raajiiv   ciTThii   likh-taa   thaa
     rajiiv-MASC   letter   write-HAB-MASC   was-MASC
     'Rajiv used to write a letter.'

    b. sariitaa   ciTThii   likh-tii   thii
      sarita-FEM   letter   write-HAB-FEM   was-FEM
      'Sarita used to write a letter.'

The Habitual marker–*t* remains constant in the present tense, as in 24, and in the Past Tense, as in 25. In its default form, the Habitual marker is–*aa* for masculine gender, as in 24a and 25a, whereas it gets inflected for feminine gender, as shown in 24b and 25b. The Habitual Aspect, as mentioned above, is a clitic on verb. It cannot be separated from the verb. No element can break up the adjacency between the verb and the Habitual Aspect marker, as shown in the ungrammaticality of example 26.

(26) * raajiiv   rah yahaaN   taa   thaa
     rajiiv   live here   HAB-MASC   was
     'Rajiv used to live here.'

3.4.3.2 Progressive Aspect

The following examples show the distribution of the Progressive Aspect marker in Hindi. As mentioned above, the Progressive Aspect marker is an independent lexical element and not a clitic on the verb (Gambhir 1981, Guru 1952, Kellogg 1938, and Kachru 1965 and 1966).

(27) a. raajiiv   ciTThii   likh   rahaa   hai
        rajiiv-MASC   letter   write   PROG-MASC   is
        'Rajiv is writing a letter.'

     b. sariitaa   ciTThii   likh   rahii   hai
        sarita-FEM   letter   write   PROG- FEM   is
        'Sarita is writing a letter.'

(28) a. raajiiv   ciTThii   likh   rahaa   thaa
        rajiiv-MASC   letter   write   PROG-MASC   was-MASC
        'Rajiv was writing a letter.'

     b. sariitaa   ciTThii   likh   rahii   thii
        sarita-FEM   letter   write   PROG-FEM   was-FEM
        'Sarita was writing a letter.'

In 27 and 28 above, the Progressive Aspect marker is *rah*. Like Habitual
Aspect markers, Progressive Aspect markers, too, carry Gender and Number
inflections. In 27a and 28a, the Progressive Aspect marker *rah* inflects for
masculine gender, whereas in 27b and 28b, it inflects for feminine gender.
Unlike the Habitual Aspect marker, other constituents, such as negation and
scrambled NPs, may come between the Progressive Aspect marker and the
verb. Let us consider the following examples:

(29) a. raajiiv   ciTThii   likh   nahiiN   rahaa   thaa
        rajiiv-MASC   letter   write   NEG   PROG-MASC   was-MASC
        'Rajiv was not writing a letter.'
        Lit: 'Rajiv was not writing a letter; maybe he was reading it.'

     b. raajiiv   likh   ciTThii   nahiiN   rahaa   thaa
        rajiiv-MASC   write   letter   NEG   PROG-MASC   was-MASC
        'Rajiv was not writing a letter.'
        Lit: 'Rajiv was writing something but not the letter.'

The example in 29a shows that a negation marker may separate the verb
stem and the progressive aspect marker. Similarly, the example in 29b shows
that a right-scrambled direct object and a negation marker can both separate
the verb stem and the Progressive Aspect marker. At this point, I do not have
an explanation as to why Habitual and Perfect Aspect both appear as clitics
on the verb whereas the Progressive Aspect appears as an independent lexical
item. However, this fact will be significant when we discuss the position of
negation in Hindi clause structure.

3.4.3.3 Perfective Aspect

The following examples show the distribution of Perfect Aspect in Hindi. As mentioned above, the Perfect Aspect marker is a clitic on the verb stem (Gambhir 1981, Guru 1952, Kellogg 1938, and Kachru 1965 and 1966).

(30) raajiiv   ghar   gay-aa
     rajiv-MASC   home   went-PERF-MASC
     'Rajiv went home.'

(31) raajiiv-ne   aam   aur   kele   khaay-e
     rajiv-ERG-SG   mango   and   bananas-MASC   ate-PERF-PL
     'Rajiv ate mangos and bananas.'

(32) sariitaa   ghar   gay-ii   hai/thii
     sariitaa-FEM home-MASC   went-PERF-FEM   is/was
     'Sarita has/had gone home.'

(33) raajiiv-ne   caay   pi-ii   hai/thii
     Rajiv- MASC-ERG   tea-FEM   drink-PERF-FEM   is/was
     'Rajiv has/had drank tea.'

The Perfect Aspect marker is the clitic–*aa* on the verb stem. It inflects for Gender, as in 30 and 32, and for Number, such as the singular in 30 and the plural in 31. Within the system of Perfect Aspect, there is a two-way distinction between the Present Perfect and the Past Perfect, as shown in 32 and 33. The example in 34, below, shows that no other constituent can separate the verb stem and the Perfect Tense marker. This will be significant when we discuss the position of negation in Hindi clause structure.

(34) * raajiiv-ne   aam   khaay-nahiiN-aa
       rajiv-ERG   mango   eat-NEG-PERF
       'Rajiv did not eat a mango.'

As discussed earlier in this chapter, Hindi has split-ergativity in terms of transitivity and Perfect Aspect. In other words, the subject is marked with Ergative Case if the verb is transitive and has a Perfect Aspect marker. The Ergative Case marker does not appear if either of these two conditions is not met. Examples such as 30 and 32 illustrate this fact. If an Ergative Case marker follows the subject, the logical subject does not control agreement, as in 31 and 33. We see that in 31 the subject, *raajiiv,* is singular, whereas the agreement on the verb is plural. This is because the plural object, *aam aur kele* 'mangos and bananas,' controls the agreement. Similarly, in 33, *raajiiv* is a masculine subject, whereas the agreement on the verb shows up as feminine for the same reason that the feminine object, *caay* 'tea,' controls the agreement. In other words, the object controls the agreement in such cases. It is worth mentioning here that any NP that is Case-marked overtly does not control agreement.

3.4.4 Mood

As far as Mood is concerned, Hindi makes a five-way distinction among the Indicative, Imperative, Subjunctive or Optative, Presumptive, and Contingent moods (Gambhir 1981, Guru 1952, and Kachru 1965 and 1966). The following examples illustrate these different types. Later in this section, I present a discussion of the Imperative and Subjunctive Moods, as they are crucial for the discussion of the syntax of negation and the licensing of negative polarity items.

Indicative:

(35) ramesh   mere   ghar   roz   aa-taa   hai
     ramesh   my   house   every day   come-HAB   is
     'Ramesh comes to my house every day.'

Imperative:

(36) tum   mere   ghar   aa-o
     you   my   house   come-IMP
     'You come to my place.'

Subjunctive:

(37) aap   mere   ghar   aa-yeN   to   mujhe   khushii   ho-gii
     you   my   house   come-SUBJ   then   to me   happiness   happen-FUT
     'I will be happy if you come to my place.'

(38) bhagwaan   aap   ko   lambii   umra   de-N
     god   you   to   long   life   give-SUBJ
     'May god give you long life.'

Presumptive:

(39) aaj   ciTThii   aa-yii   ho-gii
     today   letter   come   happen-PRESUM
     'The letter may have come today.'

Contingent:
(40) vah shaam ko aa-taa to   maiN use   kitaab de de-taa
     he evening in comes then I   to him book give give-HAB
     'I could give him the book if he comes in the evening.'

The sentences in 35 to 40 are examples of the different Moods in Hindi. In
sections 3.4.4.1 and 3.4.4.2, I present a discussion of the distribution of
Imperative and Subjunctive Moods in Hindi. The two forms of negation *mat*
and *na* 'not' occur in the Imperative and Subjunctive contexts, respectively.

3.4.4.1 Imperative

Hindi has a three-way distinction in the second person pronoun, which can
be realized as *tu* (very informal), *tum* (informal), and *aap* (formal) 'you' in
the Imperative. The following sentences illustrate the conjugation of the verb
stem with the Imperative suffixes.

(41) a. tu   aa-Ø
        you (very informal) come
        '(You) come.'

     b. tum   aa-o
        you (informal) come
        '(You) come.'

     c. aap   aa-iye
        you (formal) come
        '(You) come.'

     d. aap   mat/nahiiN/na   aa-iye
        you   NEG   come
        '(You) don't come.'

The verb stem carries three different suffixes for the three different forms of
the second person pronoun. For example, there is no suffix for the *tu* form,
as shown in 41a; the suffix for the *tum* form is–*o*, as shown in 41b; and the
suffix for the *aap* form is–*iye*, as shown in 41c. The example in 41d shows
that all three negation particles may appear in the context of the Imperative.
However, the negative marker *mat* can only occur in the context of the
Imperative. I discuss this in detail in the next chapter, which is on the syntax
of negation. The fact that the verb carries agreement markers for all forms of
the second person pronoun motivates the observation that the pronouns can
be dropped or optionally present in the sentence. Among many other pieces
of evidence, this supports the pro-drop phenomena in Hindi.

3.4.4.2 Subjunctive

The Subjunctive, or Optative, Mood in Hindi is also marked by a clitic on the verb. The Subjunctive clitics on the verb does not carry Tense or Aspectual information. They do not carry any Gender information. In other words, Subjunctives do not agree in terms of Gender. The following examples illustrate this:

(42) a. maiN   ghar   jaa-uN
         I   home   go-SUBJ
         'May I go home?'

     b. vah   ghar   ghar
         he   home   go-SUBJ
         'He may go home.'

     c. aap   ab   ghar   jaa-yeN
         you   now   home   go-SUBJ
         'You may go home now.'

     d. ve   ab   ghar   jaa-yeN
         they   now   home   go-SUBJ
         'They may go home now.'

     e. ve   ab   ghar   na   jaa-yeN
         they   now   home   NEG   go-SUBJ
         'They may not go home now.'

The examples above show that Subjunctive markers are clitics on the verb. The Subjunctive markers carry Number and Person information. In particular, the example in 41e shows that the preferred choice of the negative in the Subjunctive context is *na*. Such an example outlines the context where the negation marker *na* is used in Hindi.

3.4.5 Modals

The verbs *saknaa, paanaa, cuknaa, paRnaa,* and *caahiye* are Modals in Hindi (Gambhir 1981, Guru 1952, and Kachru 1965 and 1966). In accordance with the characteristic features of Modals, they do not occur independently. In other words, they occur with a non-finite form of a verb. Where a Modal verb is present in a sentence, the main verb occurs only in its root form, and Tense, Number, and Gender inflection appear on the Modal. The fact that the Modal carries the Tense and Aspectual clitics, including information regarding Number, Person, and Gender, is an example of edge features in Hindi. In SOV languages such as Korean and Hindi, the stacking on the

verb of various morphemes denoting grammatical relations is known as edge
feature. The following examples show the distribution of some of the modal
verbs in Hindi:

(43) a. maiN   khaa   sak-taa   huuN
        I   eat   MOD-HAB-MASC   am
        'I can eat.'

    b. sariitaa   gaa   sak-tii   hai
       I   sing   MOD-HAB-FEM   is
       'Sarita can sing.'

    c. */? sariitaa   gaa   sak   rahii   hai
       sarita   sing   MOD   PROG-FEM   is
       'Sarita can sing.'

    d. sariitaa   gaa   sak-ii
       sarita   sing   MOD-PERF-FEM
       'Sarita could sing.'

    e. sariitaa   gaa   sak-egii
       sarita   sing   MOD-FUT-FEM
       'Sarita will be able to sing.'

(44) a. maiN   mushkil   se   khaa   paa-yaa
        I   difficulty   with   eat   MOD-PERF-MASC
        'I could hardly eat.'

    b. maiN   mushkil   se   cal   pa   rahaa   huuN
       I   difficulty   with   walk   MOD-   PROG-MASC   am
       'I could hardly walk.'

(45)   maiN   khaa   cuk-aa   thaa
      I   eat   MOD-PERF-MASC   was
      'I had already eaten.'

(46) a. mujhe   ghar   jaa-naa   paR-aa
        I   home   go-INF   MOD-PERF-MASC
        'I had to go home.'

    b. mujhe   ghar   jaa-naa   caahiye
       I   home   go-INF   MOD
       'I should go home.'

The examples above show the distribution of the Modal verbs in Hindi.
The Modal verb *saknaa* 'can' is illustrated in example 43. This Modal verb

in Hindi indicates the capability of the agent of the action. As discussed above, Modals carry inflection for all Tenses and Aspects in Hindi. In 43a and 43b, the Modal carries a Present Tense and Habitual Aspect marker. It also carries information about Gender and Person, as shown in 43b. Modal verbs also carry inflections for Perfect Aspect, as in 43d, and for Future Tense, as in 43e. According to the intuitions of some speakers of Hindi, including myself, *saknaa* 'can' does not carry the Progressive Aspect marker, as shown in 43c. However, the other Modal verbs do carry the Progressive Aspect marker. Thus, the example in 44b removes the possibility of considering that Modal verbs carry inflection only when the inflections appear as clitics and do not carry inflection when the inflections appear as lexical items.

The Modal verbs *saknaa* and *paanaa* are capability markers. The Modal *cuknaa* indicates completion, whereas *paRnaa* marks compulsion. It is worth mentioning that the Modal verb *paRnaa* is different from the other three Modals previously mentioned. In the case of the other three Modals, namely *saknaa, paanaa,* and *cuknaa,* the main verb occurs in its root form. In the case of *paRnaa* and *caahiye,* however, the main verb occurs in its infinitival form, as shown in 46. Thus, to conclude, all Modal verbs carry Tense and Aspect inflections in Hindi. They do not occur in a sentence independently, that is, without the overt presence of a main verb in non-finite form.

3.5 Light Verbs

This section discusses light verbs in Hindi and will be crucial for specifically locating negation in the clause structure of Hindi. There are two types of light verbs in Hindi. They consist of either a N-V or Adj-V sequence. The first member of the light verb complex is either a noun or an adjective. Most of the time, the verb forms are either *honaa* 'to be' or *karnaa* 'to do' (Abbi 1994, Hook 1974, and Shapiro 1974). However, some light verbs may contain other verbs in the N-/Adj-V combination. A large number of light verbs consist of a noun or an adjective followed by *karnaa*, such as-*samaapt karnaa* 'to finish,' *kaam karnaa* 'to work,' *saaf karnaa* 'to clean,' and *acchaa lagnaa* 'to seem/feel good.'

(47) maiN-ne   apnaa   kaam   samaapt   kiy-aa
      I-ERG   self   work   finish   do-PERF
      'I finished my work.'

(48) pulis-ne   apnaa   kaam   kiy-aa
      police-ERG   self   work   do-PERF
      'The police did its job.'

(49) raajiiv   sariitaa se   shaadi   kar-egaa
     rajiv   sarita   with   marriage   do-FUT
     'Rajiv will marry Sarita.'

The nouns and adjectives that form part of light verbs with *karnaa* usually also appear with *honaa,*such as *samaap honaa* 'to be finished,' *khatam honaa* 'to be done,' *saaf honaa* 'to be cleaned,' *acchaa honaa* 'to be good,' *buraa honaa* 'to be bad.'

(50) meraa   kaam   samaapt   huaa
     my   work   finish   happen-PERF
     'My work is done.'

(51) aapkaa   kaam   khatam   huaa
     your   work   finish   happen-PERF
     'Did you get your job done?'

(52) kal   sariitaa ke bahan   ki shaadii   huii
     yesterday sarita   of sister   of wedding   happen-PERF
     'Sarita's sister got married yesterday.'

Light verbs consisting of nouns or adjectives with *karnaa* and light verbs with the same noun and adjective followed by *honaa* are syntactically related.[11]

    In Hindi the light verb complex does not form a syntactic unit, as there seems to be no adjacency requirement between the nominal and verbal parts of the light verb. Many different types of constituents may separate the N-/Adj-V sequence. First of all, they may be coordinated as in examples 53c and 53d.

(53) a. maiN-ne   kaam   shuru   kiy-aa
        I-ERG   work   begin   do-PERF
        'I started working.'

     b. maiN-ne   kaam   khatam   kiy-aa
        I-ERG   work   finish   do-PERF
        'I finished working.'

     c. maiN-ne   kaam   shuru   kiya   aur   khatam   kiy-aa
        I-ERG   work   begin   do-PERF   and   finish   do-PERF
        'I started working and finished it.'

     d. maiN-ne   kaam   shuru   aur   khatam   kiy-aa
        I-ERG   work   begin   and   finish   do-PERF
        'I started working and finished it.'

(54) maiN-ne   kaam   khatam to   kiy-aa. . . .
      I-ERG   work   finish FOC do-PERF
      'I did finish work.'

(55) maiN-ne   kaam   khatam bhii   kiy-aa
      I-ERG   work   finish EMPH   do-PERF
      'I finished working too.'

(56) maiN   apnaa   kaam   khatam   to   jaldii   kar-uNgaa. . . .
      I   self   work   finish   FOC   soon   do-FUT
      'I will finish my work soon.'

The examples in 54 and 56 show that some of the focus particles, namely *to,*
as in 54, and *bhii,* as in 55, can occur within the noun and the light verb
sequence. The sentence in 56 shows that both a focus particle and an adverb
can occur and separate the nominal or adjectival component and the verbal
component of the N-/Adj-V sequence.

The other constituents that can occur between the N-/Adj-V are
negation and adverbs. A discussion on the presence of negation in the
light verb construction will be particularly significant for the placement of
negation in the clause structure, and I discuss this in detail in Chapter
Three, which is on the syntax of negation. A sentence such as 57a shows
that the occurrence of a negative element such as *nahiiN* 'not' is permitted
to separate the sequence of the light verb. On the other hand, a sentence
such as 57b shows that an adverb and a negative element can both occur
in this context as well.

(57) a. maiN-ne   kaam   khatam nahiiN   kiy-aa
        I-ERG   work   finish NEG   do-PERF
        'I did not finish work.'

     b. maiN   kaam   khatam   aaj   nahiiN   kar-uNgaa. . . .
        I   work   finish   today   NEG   do-FUT
        'I will not finish the work today.'

     c. raajiiv   shaadii   sariitaa   se   nahiiN   kar-egaa
        rajiv   marriage sarita   with   NEG   do-FUT
        'Rajiv will not marry Sarita.'

     d. raajiiv   shaadii   us   se   kabhii   nahiiN   kar-egaa
        rajiv   marriage her   with sometime   NEG   do-FUT
        'Rajiv will never marry her.'

The other elements that may occur in the light verb complex are right-scrambled direct objects, right-scrambled objects with negation, and right-scrambled direct object with an adverb. In 57c *sariitaa se* 'with Sarita' is the right-scrambled direct object; in 57d *us se* 'with her' is the right-scrambled direct object, and *kabhii nahiiN* 'never' is an adverb. Thus, the nominal/adjectival component and the verbal component of the light verb sequence do not create a constituent.

3.6 Complex Clauses

Now that the properties and distribution of constituents in a simple sentence have been presented, it is important to discuss complex clauses in order to determine the location of negation in the clause structure of Hindi. In this section I address two types of complex clauses: complement clauses and infinitival clauses.

Some verbs, such as *kahnaa* 'to say,' *socnaa* 'to think,' and *samajhnaa* 'to understand,' take sentential complements. The following examples illustrate this:

(58) raajiiv-ne kahaa ki sariitaa aa rahii hai
rajiv-ERG say-PERF that sarita come PROG-FEM is
'Rajiv said that Sarita is coming.'

(59) raajiiv soc rahaa hai ki us ko sariitaa se baat karnii caahiye
rajiv think PROG is that he to sarita with talk do should
'Rajiv is thinking that he should talk to Sarita.'

(60) maiN samajh-taa huuN ki aap sabhii mujh se sahmat haiN
I understand-HAB am that you all me with agree are
'I understand that you all agree with me.'

In all three examples above, the complement clause of the verb occurs in SVO order, as the complement clause follows the verb. These are not, however, counter-examples to the canonical SOV order of Hindi sentences.

Infinitival clauses are another type of complement clause. Some Hindi verbs take an infinitival clause as their complement. *Caahnaa* 'to want' and *caahiye* 'should' are such verbs that require an infinitival clause.

(61) a. maiN inDia jaanaa caah-taa huN
I India to go want-HAB am
'I want to go to India.'

 b. mujhe inDiaa jaanaa caahiye
I-DAT India to go MOD
'I should go to India.'

The examples in 61 demonstrate that verbs such as *caahnaa* 'to want' and *caahiye* 'should' take infinitival clauses as complements, as mentioned previously. Unlike the sentential complement clauses of the type in examples 58, 59, and 60, the infinitival complement clauses do not violate the canonical object position in Hindi sentences. In other words, the infinitival clauses precede the verb, unlike sentential complements.

3.7 Adverbs

We find various types of adverbs in Hindi: time adverbs, place adverbs, manner adverbs, etc. (Kachru 1965 and 1966). These are illustrated in the following examples:

(62) a. mujhe   kal   inDiaa   jaanaa   caahiye
        I-DAT   tomorrow   India   to go   MOD
        'I should go to India tomorrow.'

     b. mujhe   yahaaN   nahiiN   aanaa   caahiye   thaa
        I-DAT   here   NEG   to come   MOD   was
        'I should not have come here.'

     c. gaaRii   dhiire-dhiire   cal-aao
        car   slow   drive-IMP
        'Drive slow.'

The adverb *kal* 'tomorrow' in 62a, *yahaaN* 'here' in 62b, and *dhiire-dhiire* 'slow' in 62c are time, place, and manner adverbs, respectively. These adverbs are not restricted with regard to their position in the sentence. They may be adjoined to any phrase they modify. However, their contribution to the meaning of a sentence or a phrase may vary depending on their position in the sentence. For more on adverbs and their relationship with functional heads see Cinque (1999). A discussion of the relative position of adverbs in a sentence is relevant for the observation that it interfaces with the licensing of negative polarity items and negation in the context of light verbs. A detailed discussion of this follows in the next chapter.

3.8 Summary

So far in this chapter I have presented a brief review of some of the typological features of Hindi and of different components of Hindi sentences. A discussion of these components is relevant for building a clause structure of Hindi. The discussion above includes most of the relevant aspects (Complementizers,

Case, Tense, Aspect, Modals, and different phrases such as NP, AP, PP, VP) of the different parts of the clause structure.

In the following section I will discuss the clause structure presented in Chomsky (1989 and 1995) and Pollock (1989), as well as the two existing proposals for Hindi clause structures (Mahajan 1990b and Kidwai 2002). Following these discussions, I will propose a clause structure of Hindi that is consistent with the empirical facts discussed above and makes correct predictions regarding the order of constituents in Hindi sentences. Such a proposal will provide a basis for location negation in the clause structure of Hindi.

4. STRUCTURE OF THE CLAUSE

There seems to be no consensus regarding the architecture of UG (universal grammar) (see Chomsky 1989). However, the structure of the clause seems to vary nevertheless. There exist disagreements among researchers in the field regarding this issue. There are three major parts of clause structure. They are the thematic layer (the VP where we have the verb and its theta marked arguments), the inflectional layer (the domain where functional projections such as AgrP, TP, or IP are projected), and the CP domain that is also called the left periphery (see Chomsky 1989, Pollock 1989, and Rizzi 1997). Under the VP Internal Subject Hypothesis, the subject of a sentence is assumed to be base generated within the vP (at the Spec, vP position; also see Huang 1993, Kuroda 1988). There has been a lot of discussion about the architecture of the clause in UG. Most discussions focus on two major questions. The first and foremost question is, What are the internal components of the functional layers? The second question, no less important, concerns the issues of the hierarchy of such projections. The fundamental basis of the relationship between elements in phrase structure is the local relationship between specifier-head and head-complement. Another question that is crucial regarding the structure of a clause is the order of the elements, particularly in the functional domain of the structure. There does not seem to be a consensus on this issue, which might be the result of parametric variation among languages. For example, Pollock (1989) assumes that TP dominates AgrP, whereas Chomsky (1989 and 1995) assumes AgrsP dominates TP.

As far as Hindi clause structure is concerned, I will address most of the issues in this section. Let us have a look at the following clause structure, as discussed in Chomsky (1989) and illustrated below in 63.

63. CP

Spec   C'   } CP Domain

   C   AgrsP

    Spec   Agrs'

     Agrs   TP

      Spec   T'

       T   NegP   Inflectional Layer

        Neg   AgroP

         Spec   Agro'

          Agro   VP

            Spec   V'   } Thematic Layer

              V   DO

The structure in 63 shows three different layers where three different types of information regarding the structure of a clause are projected. The thematic layer contains lexical information, while the functional layer contains agreement features like Tense and Aspect. In order to discuss the structure of the clause as in Chomsky's (1989 and 1995) system, I will particularly focus on two issues. I begin with the difference between Chomsky's system and that of Pollock (1989). In Chomsky's system, AgrP is split into AgrsP and AgroP. Pollock, however, presents evidence only for the presence of an AgrP. The second issue of difference between the two systems is the relative difference in the order of TP and AgrP. Pollock assumes TP dominating AgrP whereas Chomsky assumes AgrsP dominating TP as Tense stands in a government relation with the subject in tensed clauses, as can be seen from the standard subject-verb agreement phenomenon. On the basis of evidence presented in Belletti (1990), Chomsky argues that what Pollock refers to as AgrP is actually AgroP.

A point worth mentioning here is that the position of NegP is not controversial in either of the systems. Pollock (1989) assumes that the NegP is dominated by TP above AgrP, whereas Chomsky (1989 and 1995) assumes that it is in the same position, so that TP dominates the NegP above AgroP.

I turn to the structure of Hindi in detail now and will come back to the relative position of NegP in the clause structure in the next chapter.

There are at least two competing proposals concerning the clause structure of Hindi. Both proposals carry the central idea of the clause structure

64. CP

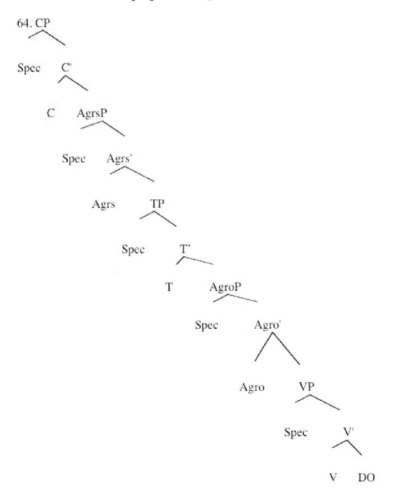

shown in 63. One argues that the AgroP is external to VP (Mahajan 1990b), whereas the other claims that the AgroP is internal to VP (Kidwai 2002). I will address the basic differences between the two proposals in detail in this section.

Mahajan (1990b) adopts the structure shown in 63, with some modifications, for the Hindi clause and provides evidence in support of his claim. The structure that Mahajan proposes for Hindi is in 64.

Mahajan's proposal is based on the object agreement phenomenon of Hindi. He argues that object agreement targets the AgroP projection and that this projection is outside VP in the functional layer. The claim that VP adverbs are adjoined to the VP supports the idea that the AgroP (where the objects moves to) is outside the VP. This proposal assumes that objects are structurally Case-marked either by V or by Agro. Non-specific objects are structurally Case-marked by V within the VP and specific objects are Case-marked by Agro. Thus, object agreement, scrambled objects, and specific DOs all target AgroP, which is located outside the VP. Let us consider the evidence that Mahajan provides in support of his claim that AgroP is outside the VP. The first piece of evidence comes from adverbial interpretation.

(65) a. pulis-ne   jaldii   se   cor   pakaR   liy-aa
          police-ERG   quickly   with   thief-MASC   catch   take-PERF-MASC
          'The police quickly arrested the thief.'

      b. pulis-ne   cor   jaldii   se   pakaR   liy-aa
          police-ERG   thief-MASC   quickly   wtih   catch   take-PERF-MASC
          'The police quickly arrested the thief.'

The interpretation of the adverb *jaldii se* 'quickly' in 65a is as an event adverb, whereas in 65b the adverb *jaldii se* 'quickly' is interpreted as a process adverb. Following Travis's (1988) suggestion that process adverbs are attached to verb projections, Mahajan concludes that the DO in 65b must be outside the VP and that the VP external position must be the Spec of VP. In cases where no agreement obtains between the object and the verb, the adverbs are ambiguous. Such an ambiguity supports his claim and obtains when the DO does not move out of the VP.

Kidwai (2002) contests Mahajan's claim and proposes that the AgroP is located inside the VP on the basis of several pieces of evidence. She claims that her proposal has certain empirical advantages. On theoretical grounds, her proposal does not violate any conditions, as the Case licensing is insensitive to the external or internal position of AgroP, whereas on empirical grounds it unifies the analysis of direct objects and indirect objects. She adopts the structure presented in 66.

66.

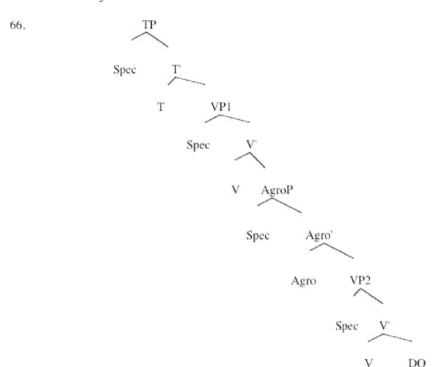

Case checking involves the raising of a constituent to enter into a checking relation with a functional head. The checking relation, for Kidwai, is very local. However, in the course of raising the subject to the Spec of AgrsP and the object to the AgroP, the DO crosses the trace of the subject. A close look at such evidence shows that in such movement of the subject to the Spec of AgrsP and the object to the AgroP, the DO does cross the trace of the subject; yet it does not violate relativized minimality, as Chomsky (1989) suggests that such movements take place under the assumptions of the equidistance condition. The shortest move condition allows movement within a minimal domain. Thus, conceptually, it makes no difference whether AgroP is internal to the VP or external to the VP.

Kidwai's proposal, as she claims, has empirical advantages as well. She argues against Mahajan's proposal, which assumes the position of AgroP to be external to the VP. Kidwai's argument against Mahajan's proposal is as follows: Mahajan claims that the scrambling of some element that creates binder is movement to the Spec of AgroP. He also assumes that only the agreeing and specific DO (DOs that are structurally Case-marked by V) can be scrambled and act as a binder for the purpose of his discussion. In other words, an element scrambled from the DO position can be an antecedent and bind some other element only if it is an agreeing DO and is structurally Case-marked by the verb. This seems problematic for Kidwai (2002). According to Kidwai, a non-agreeing, non-specific scrambled DO may co-refer with a pronominal embedded in the subject, as in 67. The following example is crucial for her argument:

(67) ek   do   laRkiyoN ko₁ unkii₁ maaeN   t₁ kuch zyaadaa hii
     one two girls   to   their   mothers   some more   EMPH
     daaNTtii haiN
     scold-HAB are

'One or two girls are scolded far too often by their mothers.' (From Kidwai 2002)

The scrambled DO *ek do laRkiyoN ko* 'one or two girls' in 67 is non-agreeing but co-refers with and binds the pronominal *unkii* 'their' that is embedded within the subject. In other words, the DO *ek do laRkiyoN ko* 'one or two girls' is structurally Case-marked, as it is a non-agreeing object and does not need to move to the Spec of AgroP. However, the example in 67 shows that the DO does scramble to the Spec of AgroP position as it binds the pronominal embedded within the subject. Again, this is inconsistent evidence against Mahajan's proposal, as the DO *ek do laRkiyoN ko* 'one or two girls' in 67, though non-agreeing, receives a specific interpretation, and under Mahajan's proposal such an interpretation comes through movement to the AgroP, which is located outside the VP.

Kidwai provides another piece of evidence that is supposed to support her argument against Mahajan's proposal. It goes as follows. There are contexts where the direct object triggers overt verb agreement, as in 68a below, or bears an overt Case marker *ko*, as in 68b, and such DOs do not receive specific interpretation. Mahajan's proposal predicts such DOs to be external to the VP. Consider the following examples:

(68) a. mujhe inaam meN kitaabeN   miliiN
        I-DAT prize in   books-FEM   get-PERF-FEM
        'I was given books in prize.'

     b. siitaa-ne ek   laRke ko   pasand kiy-aa
        sita-ERG   one boy   to   like   do-PERF
        'Sita liked a boy.'   (From Kidwai 2002)

According to Kidwai (2002), the DO *kitaabeN* 'books' in 68a agrees with the verb *miliiN* 'got' and does not receive a specific interpretation. Similarly, in 68b the DO *ek laRke ko* 'a boy' is followed by the overt Case marker *ko* but does not receive a specific interpretation. According to Kidwai, since the NPs/DOs in 68 do not receive specific interpretations, they are internal to the VP. Again, it is true that the DO in 68a agrees with the verb and the DO in 68b has an overt Case marker and also that these DOs are the objects of the perfective participle and receive specific interpretations. Under Mahajan's proposal, the specificity is a result of movement to AgroP (external to VP), so these examples have an explanation within his proposal.

To conclude, Mahajan's (1990b) proposal for the clause structure of Hindi is not problematic for the reasons Kidwai (2002) points out. Mahajan's proposal is problematic with reference to his interpretation of scrambling to L related and non-L related positions. However, his proposal does not make any claim that L related positions are also Case positions. Kidwai's argument, on the other hand, is very problematic with respect to the position of the AgroP internal to the VP. A close look at the example in 67 reveals that the scrambled DO *ek do laRkiyoN ko* 'one or two girls' is not non-specific. In other words, the DO *ek do laRkiyoN ko* 'one or two girls' obtains a specific reading. It appears to be non-specific, as it does not refer to an individual; however, it is specific in that it excludes one or two specific girls from all the rest of the girls of the world and because it talks about only a restrictive set of girls. Thus, the claims that this particular NP is internal to the VP and that the functional projection AgroP must therefore be located internally, not externally, to the VP do not hold. Similarly, in 68a and 68b, the DOs do obtain specific readings. In 68a, the DO *kitaabeN* 'books' is specific, as it refers to the books that were given as an award. In 67b, the DO *ek laRke ko* 'a boy' is also specific. Moreover, as far as the DO in 66 is concerned, Mahajan's proposal predicts its movement to an L related position (Spec, AgroP), as it bears an overt Case marker and such NPs (DOs) do not receive structural Case from the verb. In other words, since Mahajan's proposal does predict such movement, it is consistent with his proposal. The fact that DO binds the pronominal embedded within the subject shows that it moves to an L related position, namely the Spec of AgroP. Similarly, the examples in 67a and 67b are consistent with Mahajan's proposal. In 67b, the Case marker *ko* is overtly present; hence it receives a specific reading; and since it is not structurally Case-marked, it does not have any problem moving to Spec, AgroP (external to the VP). In 67a, the DO *kitaabeN* 'books' does not have an overt Case marker or a specificity marker. However, the DO is specific, as it excludes the books received as a prize from the inventory of things in the world. Thus, to summarize, it does not seem to be a sound proposal to say that AgroP, which is a functional projection, is located outside the functional layer in Hindi.

These two proposals are basically concerned with the relative structural placement of AgroP. In other words, they assume the existence of AgrP, as well as the split of AgrP as in Chomsky's (1989) proposal. In the following section, I propose a clause structure for Hindi that dispenses with the AgrP.

5. PROPOSAL: STRUCTURE OF THE HINDI SENTENCE

In this section, I propose a clause structure for Hindi. The structure that I propose is based on the VP Internal Subject Hypothesis, in which the subject originates at the Spec of vP position. The proposed structure is different from both the proposals discussed above, namely Mahajan (1990b) and Kidwai (2002), in at least two ways. First, the proposed structure dispenses with the AgrP, and, second, it is more concerned with the order of constituents in a sentence and the order of agreement morphology on the verb. One of the aims of the proposed structure is to account for the light verb construction of Hindi. I will show the detailed outline of the clause structure and its interactions with negation in the next chapter.

Following Bhatt (1999) and Rizzi (1997), I propose the structure for the Hindi sentence outlined in 69. The FP (Finiteness phrase) in my system is equivalent to the IP. From Rizzi (1997), I borrow the concept of FP. In this system, the subject of the sentence originates in the Spec of vP position. It then moves to the Spec of TP for Nominative Case-checking. Once it checks Nominative Case in this position, it moves from the Spec of TP to the Spec of FP to satisfy the EPP. I will discuss this structure in more detail below.

This structure provides a proper analysis of the placement of the subject and object in Hindi. The object stays within the VP, where it originates in the Spec of VP. The verb (V) assigns Accusative Case to its object under Spec-head relationship. In the case of non-nominative subjects—for example, Ergative and Dative subjects—the subject directly moves to the Spec of FP for EPP requirements. This move does not violate any conditions, as the Spec of TP is not available. The Spec of TP is already filled with the NP that agrees with the verb. In these instances, where subjects are already marked with non-Nominative Cases, the object, which agrees with the verb, moves to the Spec of TP position and gets Nominative Case. As mentioned earlier, only an NP in Nominative Case controls agreement. Tense is located in T, the head of TP, and the F of FP contains information regarding the finiteness or non-finiteness of the sentence. Only NPs with non-Nominative Case move to the Spec of FP.

69.

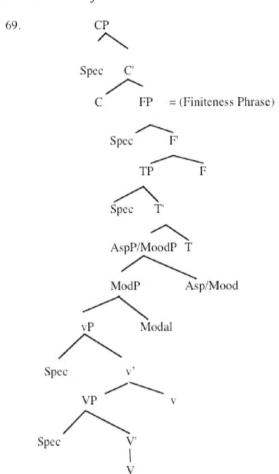

The order of morphemes in the verbal complex is as follows: The V first moves to v. Then v proceeds to Asp and incorporates the morpheme: v + Asp. Finally, v + Asp moves to T to incorporate the Tense feature.[12] The resulting affix order is verb + Aspect + Tense. This system predicts the order correctly. A discussion of the order of such verbal morphemes and their interaction with negation will follow in the next chapter. In the following examples I will show derivations of some sentences according to the proposed structure.

First of all, let us have a look at the derivation of a simple sentence. The derivation of the sentence in 70 is shown in 71.

(70) raajiiv   aaam   khaataa   hai
     rajiv   mango   eat-HAB   is
     'Rajiv eats a mango.'

71.

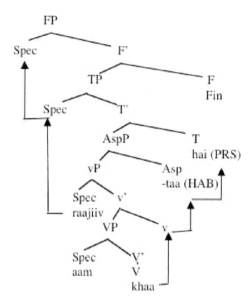

In 71, the subject *raajiiv* originates in the Spec of vP position and then moves to the Spec of TP to check Nominative Case. It then moves further to the Spec of FP to satisfy the EPP. Tense is located at the head position of TP. The object remains in situ, as it receives Accusative Case from the verb in the Spec-head configuration. The verb *khaa* moves to the v and then to the Asp position, where it gets the Habitual Aspect morpheme. Finally, v + Asp moves to the T, where it receives Tense, in this case Present.

Now let us have a look at the example in 72, which deals with the non-Nominative subject, and the corresponding structure in 73.

(72) raajiiv-ne   ciTThii   likh-ii   thii
     rajiv-ERG   letter   write-PERF   was
     'Rajiv had written a letter.'

In 73, once the subject *raajiiv* is already Case-marked with Ergative Case *ne*, it does not move to a position where structural Cases are checked. It instead moves to the Spec of FP to check the EPP. On the other hand, the verb in such cases (Ergative or Dative) is not a structural Case assigner. Hence, in 73, the object *ciTThii* 'letter' moves to the Spec of TP to get structural Case (Nominative). From this position, the object seems to agree with tense in the head of TP. The Ergative subject does not agree with Tense, as it is a Postpositional phrase, and in this case the NP in Ergative Case does not land

73.

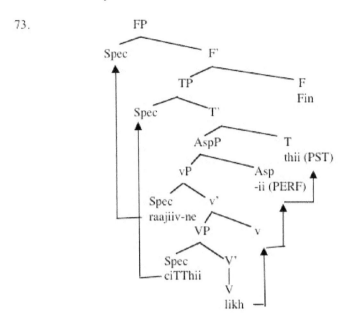

in the Spec of TP anyway, as it is not filled by the object. This structure predicts that the element in the Spec of TP will agree with the Tense and not with any other element. The agreement morphemes on the verb get there by head movement–incorporation, as in 71 above: the verb first moves to v, then gets an Aspectual morpheme in Asp, and from there moves to T for the Tense marker *thii* 'was.'

I would now like to move on to discuss default agreement in the following examples, 74 and 75. In this case, neither the subject nor the object agrees with the verb. When the subject is marked either Ergative or Dative, and a specificity marker *ko*, which is also a Case marker, follows the object, then the verb carries a default agreement marker.

(74) siimaa-ne   sariitaa   ko   dekh-aa   thaa
       sima-ERG-FEM   sarita-FEM   Spec   see-PERF-MASC   was-MASC
       'Sima had seen Saritaa.'

In 74, the subject NP and the object NP are both followed by overt Case markers (postpositions). The subject *siimaa* is followed by the postposition *ne*, which is an Ergative Case marker, whereas the object *sariitaa* is followed by the postposition *ko*, which is both the specificity marker and the Accusative marker. Since both the NPs carry overt Case markers, neither of

75.

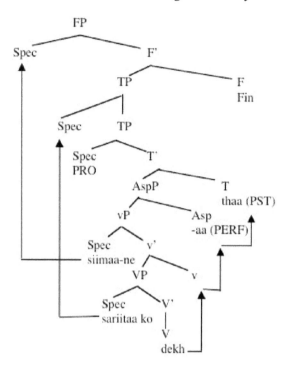

them can agree with the verb. The verb carries a default agreement marker, i.e. third person singular and masculine, as it always does in such cases. Also, since the object NP carries an overt Case marker, it does not move to the Spec of TP; rather, it is adjoined to TP. For the purpose of the default Case mechanism, I assume the presence of a PRO in the Spec of TP that exhibits agreement with the verb.

This analysis of Hindi clause structure also makes the prediction that agreeing objects do move out of the VP contra Kidwai (2002). The agreeing objects move to the Spec of TP position. Hence, Kidwai's analysis, assuming the location of objects within the VP, does not capture empirical generalizations about Hindi. The structure that I have proposed captures the empirical generalizations. I show more implications and advantages of this proposed structure in the next chapter, where I show the interaction of negation and other constituents, particularly light verbs, in clause structure.

6. SCRAMBLING OPERATION IN HINDI

I have shown earlier in this chapter that the word order in a sentence with a transitive verb is S-DO-V and that it is S-IO-DO-V in a sentence with a di-transitive verb. However, we do find some other word orders in Hindi as well. The phenomenon is known as scrambling. It is very important to consider the phenomenon of scrambling for a discussion of the syntax of negation and the licensing of negative polarity items in Hindi.

The word order in Hindi is not fixed (strict), as in English; it is relatively free. Other orders are possible in addition to SOV. Thus, a simple sentence like 76 can have the various word order possibilities shown below, resulting from scrambling.

(76) a. ravi-ne   sariita   ko   kapRe   di-ye
      ravi-ERG   sarita   to   clothes   give-PERF

     b. sariitaa   ko   ravi-ne   kapRe   di-ye
       sarita   to   ravi-ERG   clothes   give-PERF

     c. ravi-ne   kapRe   di-ye   sariitaa   ko
      ravi-ERG   clothes   give-PERF   sarita   to

     d. kapRe   di-ye   ravi-ne   sariitaa   ko
      clothes   give-PERF   ravi-ERG   sarita   to

     e. kapRe   di-ye   sariitaa   ko   ravi-ne
      clothes   give-PERF   sarita   to   ravi-ERG

     'Ravi gave clothes to Sarita.'

The examples in 76 show some of the word order possibilities as a result of scrambling operation. Whereas 76a is canonical order, 76b shows the scrambling of IO *sariitaa ko* over the subject *ravi ne*. The rightward scrambling of the IO is shown in 76c. The rightward scrambling of both subject and IO is shown in 76d, whereas the last example, in 76e, shows the rightward scrambling of first the subject and then the IO.

There are two types of scrambling operations: argument shift and XP adjunction (Mahajan 1994). The examples in 77 show the argument shift. In 77b, the DO is scrambled over the subject. The DO *kaun sii baat* moves to the Spec of AgroP, whereas the subject, which is followed by the morphological Case (Ergative) marker, remains inside the VP. This is structurally represented in 77c.

(77) a. raajiiv-ke   bhaai-ne   *kaun sii*   *baat*   nahiiN   maan-ii
      rajiv-GEN   brother-ERG   which-one   thing   NEG   obey-PERF

     b. *kaun sii*   *baat*   raajiiv   ke   bhaai-ne   nahiiN   maan-ii
      which-one   thing   rajiv   GEN   brother-ERG   NEG   obey-PERF

     'What did Rajiv's brother not obey?'

(77) c.

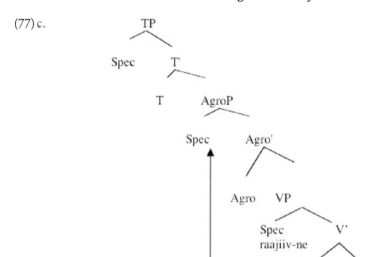

The examples in 78 outline XP adjunction. The canonical word order of Hindi is shown in 78a, whereas the example in 78b shows the long-distance scrambling of the reflexive *apne app se,* to be adjoined to the higher IP. The structural representation of 78b is given in 78c.

(78) a. sariitaa-ko   lag-taa   hai ki   raajiiv *apne aap se* ghRinaa kar-taa   hai
          sarita-DAT think-HAB is   that raajiv self with   hate   do-HAB   is

      b. *apne aap se* sariitaa-ko lag-taa   hai ki   raajiiv ghRinaa kartaa hai
          self with   sarita-DAT think-HAB is   that rajiv   hate   do-HAB is

      'Sarita thinks that Rajiv hates himself.'

In 78b, the reflexive DO *apne aaap se* is scrambled long-distance across the main clause, as diagrammed in 78c. This, according to Mahajan (1994), is an example of adjunction to a maximal phrase (XP), as well as an example of XP-adjunction and A-bar scrambling. A-bar scrambled elements do not need Case.

As mentioned above, there are two distinct syntactic operations with the scrambling phenomenon (Mahajan 1994): argument shift (an operation that shifts an NP into the specifier position of a functional projection other than C) and XP adjunction (movement to a non–L related position). The scrambling effects mentioned above are not restricted to simple sentences. They extend to more complex structures, including embedded non-finite

(78) c.

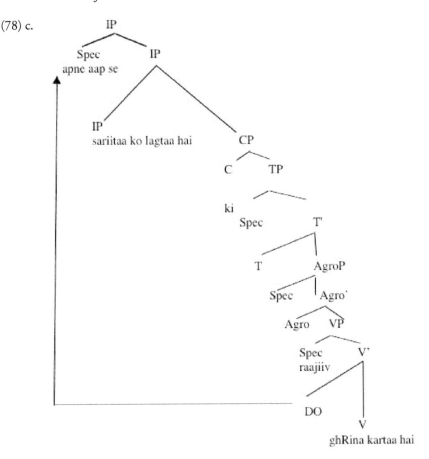

clauses. For example, the argument of an embedded non-finite clause may scramble with the arguments of the matrix clause.

(79) a. ravi-ne   sariitaa se *suman kaa saamaan kamare me rakhne ko* kahaa
    ravi-ERG sarita   to suman of   things   room   in   put   to say-PREF

b. sariitaa se *suman kaa saamaan kamare me rakhne ko* ravi ne kahaa

c. sariitaa se *suman kaa saamaan* ravi ne *kamare me rakhne ko* kahaa

'Ravi told Sarita to keep Suman's luggage in the room.'

In 79b, the entire infinitival clause is scrambled to the left. The example in 79c shows further complications in the scrambling phenomenon, as only a part of the infinitival clause is scrambled to the left, where 79a is the basic word order.

Having discussed both local and long-distance scrambling, I address in the following section the interaction of scrambling with Binding, WCO, quantifier scope, and conditions on movement. A detailed discussion of the interaction of scrambling with the other syntactic phenomena just mentioned is crucial for setting up the discussion on the licensing of negative polarity items in Chapters Four and Five.

6.1 Scrambling and Binding

The interaction of scrambling and Binding provides support in favor of the argument that Hindi scrambling targets both A and A-bar positions (Mahajan 1990b).

An antecedent binds a reflexive from an argument position (Chomsky 1981). Keeping this in mind, consider the following two examples, in which scrambling targets an argument position:

(80) a. * apne$_i$ maalik-ne ek   naukar$_i$ naukri se   nikaal di-yaa
         self's boss-ERG one   servant service from dismiss give-PERF
         'Self's boss dismissed a servant.'

     b. ? ek naukar$_i$ apne$_i$ maali-ne naukri se nikaal di-yaa

The reflexive in 80a is ungrammatical, as the antecedent does not bind the reflexive. The DO in 80b has moved to the VP external position, whereas the subject is still VP internal. This follows from the assumption that object agreement is accomplished by movement of the object to the Spec of AgroP. Scrambling of the DO changes the binding possibilities. In other words, the antecedent *ek naukar* can in this case bind the reflexive *apne*. Because antecedents can bind reflexives only from argument positions, the target position of scrambling in 80b must be an argument position.

Reconstruction of an element is possible from an A-bar position only. Keeping this in mind, let us have a look at the following example, in which scrambling targets an A-bar position:

(81) a. raam$_i$ apne aap ko$_i$ pasand kar-taa   hai
         ram   self   to   like   do-HAB   is
         'Ram likes himself.'

     b. apne aap ko$_i$ raam$_i$ pasand t$_i$ kartaa hai

(82) apne aap ko$_i$ siitaa soctii   hai ki   raam$_i$ pasand t$_i$ kar-taa   hai
     self   to Sita think-HAB is that ram   like   do-HAB   is
     'Sita thinks that Ram likes himself.'

In 81b and 82, the reflexive *apne aap ko* is scrambled from its canonical DO position. In 81b, the reflexive *apne aap ko* is the DO of the matrix clause, whereas in 82 the reflexive *apne aap ko* is the DO of the embedded clause. The scrambling in 81b is local, whereas in 82, the scrambling is long-distance. However, both are still interpreted as bound by their respective antecedents. This binding is argued to be possible under the assumptions of reconstruction. In other words, the scrambled, reflexive DO *apne aap ko* in both 81b and 82 reconstructs back to the position it originated in for reflexive interpretation and is bound by its antecedent, *raam,* in both examples. Because the reconstruction of a particular element is possible from A-bar positions only, Mahajan argues that scrambling targets A-bar positions as well as A-positions.[13]

6.2 Scrambling and Weak Crossover

The interaction between scrambling and WCO also provides support in favor of the argument that scrambling in Hindi targets both A and A-bar positions. WCO is a diagnostic for determining the nature of the landing site of movement. Scrambling to an A-position overrides WCO effects, whereas scrambling to an A-bar position does not override WCO effects (Mahajan 1994). In other words, WCO can be overridden from an A position but not from an A-bar position. Consider the following examples, illustrating these facts. In example 83, the pronominal and the variable are in a classical WCO configuration.

(83) * [. . . . Operator$_i$ [[. . . . pronoun$_i$. . . .]. . . . .variable$_i$. . . .]]

The sentences in 84 and 85 show WCO in Hindi.

(84) ?? us ke$_i$ maalik-ne   kaun si kitaab$_i$ pheNk dii
         its   owner-ERG   which   book   throw   give-PERF
         'Which book did its owner throw away?'

(85) ??? us ke$_i$ maalik-ne   sab   kitaabeN$_i$ pheNk diiN
          its   owner-ERG   all   books   throw   give-PERF
          'Its owner threw away all the books.'

The scrambling of the DO overrides the WCO effects in 86 and 87.

(86) kaun si kitaab$_i$ us ke$_i$ maalik-ne   pheNk dii
         which   book   its   owner-ERG   throw   give-PERF
         'Which book did its owner throw away?'

(87) sab   kitaabeN$_i$ us ke$_i$ maalik-ne   pheNk   dii
     all   books   its   owner-ERG   throw   give-PERF
     'Its owner threw away all the books.'

Thus, the scrambling of the DO in 86 and 87 are in A positions as they override WCO effects. On the other hand, long-distance scrambling does not override WCO (Déprez 1989). This shows that the LD scrambling targets A-bar positions, as shown in 88.

(88) * kis-ko$_i$ uskii$_i$ maaN   soctii hai   ki   anu   t$_i$ pyaar   kartii   hai
     whom   his   mother think-HAB   that anu   love   do-HAB   is
     'Who is such that his mother thinks that Anu loves him?'

However, the issue of whether local scrambling in Hindi overrides WCO effects is controversial. On the basis of the judgments in 86 and 87, Mahajan (1994) argues that the scrambled positions in those examples are A positions, but these data are controversial. Some native speakers of Hindi do not accept the interpretations in 86 and 87. Thus, I suggest that the target positions in 86 and 87 are A-bar positions, as the WCO effect is not overridden.

6.3 Scrambling and Quantifier Scope

On the basis of the interaction of scrambling and quantifier scope, Déprez (1989) notes another significant distinction between local and long-distance scrambling with regard to the positions they target. Local scrambling allows floating quantifiers in any of the positions to which the NPs can be scrambled. This is shown in the following examples in Hindi:

(89) a. raam-ne   mohan   ko   [saarii   kitaabeN]   lau-taa   diiN
       raam-ERG   mohan   to   all   books   return-PERF   give-PERF
       'Ram returned all the books to Mohan.'

     b. raam-ne   kitaabeN$_i$ mohan   ko   [saarii t$_i$]   lau-taa   diiN

     c. kitaabeN$_i$ raam-ne   mohan   ko   [saarii t$_i$]   lau-taa   diiN

     d. kitaabeN$_i$ raam-ne   [saarii t$_i$]   mohan   ko   lau-taa   diiN

The examples in 89 show the scrambling of the NP out of the QP (Quantifier phrase). Following Sportiche (1988), where the quantifier is analyzed as being generated inside the NP, Déprez shows, in 89, that quantifiers may move with the head and be stranded at any position to which the NP scrambles. She concludes that the quantifier stranding is a property of local scrambling, which targets an A position. On the other hand, quantifier stranding is not a property of long-distance scrambling, as it targets an A-bar position. The ungrammaticality of the example in 90 shows this fact.

(90) * [phal$_i$ raam samajh-taa   hai ki [[saare t'$_i$]$_i$ anu jaan-tii   hai
         fruit   raam understands-HAB is   that all   anu know-HAB is

[ki t$_i$ mohan khaa   gayaa]]]
that mohan eat-PERF give-PERF
'Ram understands that Mohan knows that Anu ate all the fruits.'

In 90 the entire NP moves first to the pre-subject position in the intermediate clause. When the head of the NP moves farther up, leaving the quantifier in the intermediate position, the sentence becomes ungrammatical. This shows that the two different types of scrambling target two different positions.

6.4 Scrambling and Conditions on Movement

In order to complete the discussion on scrambling, I will briefly discuss long-distance movement of wh-phrases in Hindi. The examples of long-distance movement of wh-phrases below show that they are not instances of argument shift, which are subject to locality condition, as the landing sites of the LD-moved wh-phrase do not override WCO violations, as shown in example 91.

(91) * kaun   sa   aadmii$_i$ apni$_i$ bahin-ne   soc-aa
          which   one   man   self's sister-ERG(SUB) think-PERF

ki   raam-ne   t$_i$ dekh-aa   thaa
that   ram-ERG (SUB)   see-PERF   was

* 'Which man did self's sister think that Ram had seen?'

Extended chain formation is not possible for movement of an NP out of a finite clause. Thus, such movements do not form L-chains, and the landing site of such movement is a non–L related position. Although Mahajan (1994) claims that the local movement of wh-phrases overrides WCO violations, such is not the case. As I pointed out, some native Hindi speakers do not agree with Mahajan's judgments regarding the examples in 86 and 87. It therefore seems to be the case that even local movement of wh-phrases targets an A-bar position.

According to Mahajan (1994), scrambling in Hindi shows two clearly distinct operations: argument shift (to L positions) and adjunction (to non–L positions). Argument shift exhibits the properties of A movement, whereas adjunction exhibits the properties of A-bar movement. On the other hand, Srivastav (1994) and Kidwai (2002) show that there is strong evidence available for the argument that scrambling in Hindi targets only A-bar positions.

7. CONCLUSION

This chapter began with the introduction in first section followed by the presentation of a brief review of the typological characteristics of Hindi in the second section. The third section gave a detailed description of various components of Hindi sentences. In the fourth section, the internal structure, along with descriptions, of some of the phrases, such as NP, VP, PP, and AP, was discussed. After a detailed outline of the various constituents and their structure was given, a discussion of the structure of the UG clause and two earlier proposals for the clause structure of Hindi (namely Mahajan 1990b and Kidwai 2002) were presented in the fourth section. In the fifth section, finally, my proposal for the structure of the Hindi sentence was outlined. My proposal dispenses with the assumption of the existence of AgrP in the clause and has implications for the location of negation phrases (to follow in the next chapter). This section also explained the notion of Nominative and non-Nominative subjects in Hindi. In the sixth section, in addition to discussing the structure, I briefly discuss the scrambling operation in Hindi and its interaction with various other syntactic phenomena; these are relevant for the discussions to follow in that the analysis of the licensing of negative polarity items depends on the interaction of binding principles and scrambled phrases. In the next chapter, on the syntax of negation, I explore the location of the negation phrase in the Hindi clause structure proposed in this chapter.

Chapter Three
Syntax of Negation in Hindi: Description and Representation

1. INTRODUCTION

Working from the structure I proposed in Chapter Two, this chapter mainly aims at locating negation in the clause structure of Hindi.

Kachru (1965) presents the first linguistic description of negation in Hindi in a brief discussion of the derivation of negative sentences. Her analysis gives an account of the relationship between the negative particle and other constituents of the sentence. She also discusses negative prefixes and pre- and post-verbal negation in Hindi. From that time, several others have worked on negation in Hindi as well. Bhatia (1978) presents a description of the syntax and semantics of negation in six South Asian languages, including Hindi, observing that the surface distribution of negation is semantically (and not morphologically) conditioned. A short description of negation in Hindi is also available in Mohanan (1994) and Dwivedi (1991). Dwivedi argues that negation heads its own maximal projection as NegP.

The purpose of this chapter is to present a detailed description of negation in Hindi, as stated above. It also aims to discuss several other issues related to negation, such as the difference between sentential negation and constituent negation and their structural positions. The issues that will be discussed in this chapter are the following: first of all, I present a description of the distribution of negation markers in Hindi. I also elaborate on the different positions of negation in clause structure (i.e. negation in different tenses, imperative sentences, and, finally, the interaction of negation with light verbs). The second issue that I discuss in this chapter is the question of sentential and constituent negation. In this section I present evidence in support of the pre-verbal negative marker as a marker of sentential negation and

argue that sentential negation is located outside the VP, while constituent
negation appears in adjoined positions. On the basis of the discussion proposed above, I will draw conclusions about the position of sentential negation in the clause structure of Hindi. Negation heads its own maximal
projection in Hindi, and it is located in the functional domain outside the
VP. Finally, I discuss other ways of expressing negation in Hindi in the
absence of a negative marker.

2. NEGATIVE MARKERS

Negation in Hindi is expressed through three negation markers: *nahiiN, na,*
and *mat.* Of these three, *nahiiN* is used most frequently. I will discuss the
occurrence of all three elements of negation in this section.

Let us consider the following examples in 1:

(1) a.   maiN   *nahiiN / ?na / *mat*   khaa-uNgaa
          I   NEG   eat-FUT
          'I will not eat.'

     b.   hamlog   kahaaN   *na / nahiiN / *mat*   jaa-yeN
          we   where   NEG   go-SUBJ
          'Where should we not go?'

     c.   mandir   ke   andar   tasviir   *na/nahiiN/ mat*   le-N
          temple   of   inside picture   NEG   take-SUBJ
          'Please do not take pictures inside the temple.'

     d.   *mat/na/nahiiN*   khaa-o
          NEG   eat-IMP
          'Do not eat.'

The three negatives are shown in 1. It is important to mention here
that *nahiiN* can be used in most of the cases. However, the use of the other
two negatives, namely *na* and *mat,* is restricted. *Na* is used in Subjunctive
and Imperative cases, as in 1b and 1d, whereas the use of *mat* is restricted to
Imperative sentences, as shown in 1d. Example 1c shows that *mat* can also be
used in Subjunctive contexts. This is because the Subjunctive example in 1c
is equally good as an Imperative. If a Subjunctive sentence can be interpreted
as a request or command, then the use of *mat* in such cases is allowed. If the
interpretation of the Subjunctive sentence is not a request or command, then
the use of *mat* is not permitted, as shown in 1b. The ungrammatical use of
na in 1a as opposed to 1 (b–d) shows that it is restricted to Subjunctive and

Imperative sentences only. However, the use of *na* is the preferred choice only in the Subjunctive.

The negative *nahiiN* can be used in all the cases mentioned above, as *nahiiN* is the marker that occurs most frequently in Hindi. The negative marker *nahiiN* is actually a compound of the negation marker *na* and the emphatic marker particle *hiiN* 'only.'[1] Thus, it seems to be a possibility that *na* is the underlying negative marker, and the other forms are the result of some significant historical development over a period of time. However, the emergence of the other negative marker, *mat,* is not clear, and, historically, there does not seem to be any relationship between *mat* and the form *na*. Thus, there does not seem to be any evidence for the above- stated assumption.

3. NEGATION IN HINDI: A DESCRIPTION

In this section I will present a description of negation and the distribution of negative markers in the three Tenses, the three Aspects, and in Imperative sentences, Modal verbs, and with light verbs. Thus, this section presents the interaction of negation markers with the various aspects of Hindi sentences discussed in Chapter Two.

3.1. Negation and Tense

Negation occurs with all three Tenses in Hindi: Present, Past, and Future. A closer look at the interaction of negation with each is crucial for locating negative markers in the clause structure of Hindi. In this section I will only talk about *nahiiN*. I will discuss the other two, *na* and *mat,* in the following sections of this chapter, as the negative marker *mat* is restricted to Imperatives and *na* is restricted mainly to Subjunctives.

3.1.1 Negation in Present Tense (Non-Verbal Predicates)

In this section, I give a description of negation with non-verbal predicates in the Present Tense, as shown in 2. I contrast each occurrence of negation in a sentence with an affirmative sentence. In a simple Present Tense sentence, the negative marker precedes the Tense marker. It is never the case that the negative marker follows the tense marker.[2] Brief discussions of the placement of negation and tense are available in Bhatia (1978), Gambhir (1981), Guru (1952), Kellogg (1938), and Kachru (1965 and 1966). In the following examples, the negative markers also precede the auxiliaries. The auxiliaries are different Present Tense forms of the verb honaa 'be,' agreeing with the subject. The data shows not only the occurrence of negative markers in Present Tense, but also the agreement between the subject and the auxiliaries.

(2) a. maiN   DaakTar   huuN
        I   doctor   am
        'I am a doctor.'

     b. maiN   DaakTar   nahiiN   huuN
        I   doctor   NEG   am
        'I am not a doctor.'

     c. tum   DaakTar   ho
        you-MASC/FEM-SG/PL   doctor   are
        'You are a doctor.'

     d. tum   DaakTar   nahiiN   ho
        you-MASC/FEM-SG/PL   doctor   NEG   are
        'You are not a doctor.'

     e. aap   DaakTar   haiN
        you-MASC/FEM-SG/PL   doctor   are
        'You are a doctor.'

     f. aap   DaakTar   nahiiN   haiN
        you-MASC/FEM-SG/PL   doctor   NEG   are
        'You are not a doctor.'

     g. vah   DaakTar   hai
        s/he   doctor   is
        'S/he is a doctor.'

     h. vah   DaakTar   nahiiN   hai
        s/he   doctor   NEG   is
        'S/he is not a doctor.'

     i. ve   DaakTar   haiN
        they-MASC/FEM   doctor   are
        'They are doctors.'

     j. ve   DaakTar   nahiiN   haiN
        they-MASC/FEM   doctor   NEG   are
        'They are not doctors.'

In the examples in 2, I first give an affirmative sentence and then a negative parallel to show the relative position of the negation markers. Thus, the examples in b, d, f, h, and j are the negative sentences, containing the negation marker *nahiiN*. In all these examples, the negation marker precedes the Present Tense markers.[3] The tense markers are not optional in this context, unlike Present Habitual, which is discussed later in this chapter.

3.1.2 Negation in Past Tense (Non-Verbal Predicate)

In this section, I present a description of negation in Past Tense, particularly with non-verbal predicates. In example 3, I contrast each occurrence of negation in a sentence with its occurrence in the corresponding affirmative sentence. Just as in the Present Tense cases in , the negative marker precedes the Past Tense verb in a simple Past Tense sentence. The negative markers also precede the auxiliaries in all the Numbers, Genders, and Persons (Bhatia 1978, Gambhir 1981, Guru 1952, Kellogg 1938, and Kachru 1965 and 1966). In the examples in 3, the auxiliaries are various Past Tense forms of the verb *honaa* 'be,' agreeing with the subjects and showing negation in Past Tense. It is usually not the case that the negative marker follows the Past Tense verb with a sentential negation interpretation.

(3) a. maiN   DaakTar   thaa
         I   doctor   was
         'I was a doctor.'

     b. maiN   DaakTar   nahiiN   thaa
         I   doctor   NEG   was
         'I was not a doctor.'

     c. tum   DaakTar   the
         you-MASC-SG/PL   doctor   were
         'You were a doctor.'

     d. tum   DaakTar   nahiiN   the
         you-MASC-SG/PL   doctor   NEG   were
         'You were not a doctor.'

     e. aap   DaakTar   the
         you-MASC-SG/PL   doctor   were
         'You were a doctor.'

     f. aap   DaakTar   nahiiN   the
         you-MASC-SG/PL   doctor   NEG   were
         'You were not a doctor.'

     g. tum   DaakTar   thii
         you-FEM-SG/PL   doctor   were
         'You were a doctor.'

h. tum   DaakTar   nahiiN   thii
   you-FEM-SG/PL   doctor   NEG   were
   'You were not a doctor.'

i. aap   DaakTar   thiiN
   you-FEM-SG/PL   doctor   were
   'You were a doctor.'

j. aap   DaakTar   nahiiN   thiiN
   you-FEM-SG/PL   doctor   NEG   were
   'You were not a doctor.'

k. vah   DaakTar   thaa
   he   doctor   was
   'He was a doctor.'

l. vah   DaakTar   nahiiN   thaa
   he   doctor   NEG   was
   'He was not a doctor.'

m. ve   DaakTar   the
   they-MASC   doctor   were
   'They were doctors.'

n. ve   DaakTar   nahiiN   the
   they-MASC   doctor   NEG   were
   'They were not doctors.'

The examples given above in 3 show affirmative sentences, (a, c, e, g, i, k, m), followed by their negative counterparts, in (b, d, f, h, j, l, n), and give the systematic distribution of negation markers in the non-verbal predicates of the Past Tense in Hindi. In all the negative examples, it is evident that the negation marker *nahiiN* precedes the non-verbal Past Tense marker. It is also clear that Tense markers are not optional in the Past Tense.

I would like briefly to touch on here the different forms of the verb *honaa* 'be' in the Past Tense. There is no distinct marker for first person in the Past Tense, unlike in the Present Tense. There is a clear four-way division in terms of Number and Gender, namely *thaa* (masculine singular), *the* (masculine plural), *thii* (feminine singular), and *thiiN* (feminine plural). Even for the second person *tum,* there is no distinct marker, unlike in the Present Tense. That is to say, we have the Present Tense marker *ho* for the second person *tum,* whereas in the Past Tense there is no specific marker for *tum;* the form of the second person *tum* is the same in both singular and plural. It is worth mentioning, however, that in the case of *tum,* singular or plural, the agreement in the Past Tense is plural in the masculine, as in 3d, and singular in the feminine, as in 3h.

Past Tense agreement in Hindi is different from Present Tense agreement in the sense that Past Tense displays gender agreement in addition to number agreement.

3.1.3 Negation in Future Tense

Negation in the context of Future Tense is similar to its context in the Present and Past Tense in terms of its position in a sentence. In other words, the negative marker in Future Tense precedes the verb in the sentence (Bhatia 1978, Gambhir 1981, Guru 1952, Kellogg 1938, and Kachru 1965 and 1966) as it does in the Present and Past Tenses.

(4) a. maiN   aam   khaa-uNgaa
         I   mango   eat-FUT-I-MASC
         'I will eat mango.'

     b. maiN   aam   nahiiN   khaa-uNgaa
         I   mango   NEG   eat-FUT-I-MASC
         'I will not eat mango.'

     c. tum   aam   khaa-oge
         you-MASC-SG/PL   mango   eat-FUT-II-SG/PL
         'You (m) will eat mango.'

     d. tum   aam   nahiiN   khaa-oge
         you-MASC-SG/PL   mango   NEG   eat-FUT-II-SG/PL-MASC
         'You (m) will not eat mango.'

     e. aap   aam   khaa-yeNge
         you-MASC-SG/PL   mango   eat-FUT-IISG/PL-MASC
         'You (m) will eat mango.'

     f. aap   mango   nahiiN   khaa-yeNge
         you-MASC-SG/PL   mango   NEG   eat-FUT-IISG/PL-MASC
         'You (m) will not eat mango.'

     g. tum   aam   khaa-ogii
         you-FEM-SG   mango   eat-FUT-IISG-FEM
         'You (f) will eat mango.'

     h. tum   aam   nahiiN   khaa-ogii
         you-FEM-SG   mango   NEG   eat-FUT-IISG-FEM
         'You (f) will not eat mango.'

     i. aap   aam   khaa-yeNgii
         you-FEM-SG/PL   mango   eat-FUT-IISG/PL-FEM
         'You (f) will eat mango.'

     j. aap   aam   nahiiN   khaa-yeNgii
         you-FEM-SG/PL   mango   NEG   eat-FUT-IISG/PL-FEM
         'You (f) will not eat mango.'

k. vah   aam   khaa-yehii
    she   mango   eat-FUT-IIISG-FEM
    'She will eat mango.'

l. vah   aam   nahiiN   khaa-yehii
    she   mango   NEG   eat-FUT-IIISG-FEM
    'She will not eat mango.'

m. ve   aam   khaa-yeNge
    they-MASC   mango   eat-FUT-PL-MASC
    'They will eat mango.'

n. ve   mango   nahiiN   khaa-yeNge
    they-MASC   mango   NEG   eat-FUT-PL-MASC
    'They will not eat mango.'

o. aaj   varshaa   ho-gii
    today   rain   happen-FUT-FEM-IIISG
    'It will rain today.'

p. aaj   varshaa   nahiiN   ho-gii
    today   rain   NEG   happen-FUT-FEM-IIISG
    'It will not rain today.'

q.

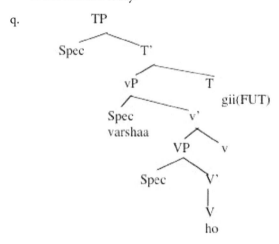

The examples above in 4 (a–p) show the position of the negation marker in the context of Future Tense. Once again, I give the affirmative examples first, and the respective negative counterparts follow. The examples show that, just like in Present and Past Tense non-verbal predicates, the negation marker in the Future Tense (verbal predicate) also precedes the verb. The structure in 4q shows the position of Tense in the clause structure.

The tense morphology in the Future Tense is different from that in the Present and Past Tenses. First of all, a form of the verb *honaa* 'be' is not present as an auxiliary in Future Tense sentences. The verb *honaa* 'be' is treated as a main verb in the Future Tense. The Future Tense marker in Hindi is a combination of the Subjunctive marker and the Future Tense marker. In other words, the root that shows the Future Tense marker in Hindi is not the bare root form of the main verb; rather, it is the Subjunctive form of the verb that receives the Future Tense morpheme. I discussed the Subjunctive morphology in the previous chapter. The agreement system is, nevertheless, preserved. An agreement marker occurs at the right-most edge of the Future Tense marker. In Hindi, the agreement markers, according to Number and Gender, are as follows:–*aa* (masculine singular),–*e* (masculine plural),–*ii* (feminine singular), and–*iiN* (feminine plural).

3.2 Negation and Aspect

This section discusses the occurrence of negation in the context of Aspect. I specifically discuss the occurrence and distribution of negation with reference to Habitual Aspect, Progressive Aspect, and Perfect Aspect.

3.2.1 Negation in Habitual Aspect

The Habitual Aspect marker in Hindi is–*t*. It is a clitic on the verb. Number and Gender morphemes occur to the right of the Aspect marker. As far as the interaction of the Habitual Aspect marker and negation is concerned, the negative marker precedes the entire verbal complex in the case of sentential negation, as in 5b, and follows the entire verbal complex (a fully inflected verb with the number, person, gender, and agreement morphemes) in the case of constituent negation (a discussion of the phenomenon of constituent negation follows in the next section), as in 5d. Since the morphology of the verb is a complex of several clitics, there is a strict adjacency requirement between them, as the ungrammaticality of 5e shows. The example in 5a is the affirmative counterpart of 5b. In other words, 5e shows that no element can disrupt the adjacency between the verb stem and the Aspect marker.

(5) a. maiN   skuul   jaa-taa   huuN/thaa
       I   school   go-HAB-MASC   am/was
       'I go/used to go to school.'

    b. maiN   skuul   nahiiN   jaa-taa   (?huuN)
       I   school   NEG   go-HAB-MASC   am
       'I do not go to school.'

c. maiN   skuul   nahiiN   jaa-taa   *(thaa)
   I   school NEG   go-HAB-MASC   was
   'I do not go to school.'

d. maiN   skuul   jaa-taa   nahiiN   (constituent negation)
   I   school go-HAB-MASC   NEG
   'I do not go to school.'

e. * maiN   skuul   jaa-t- nahiiN-aa
     I   school go-HAB-NEG-MASC
     'I do not go to school.'

f.

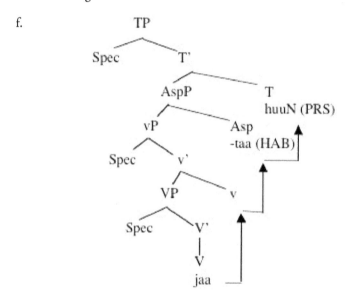

The structure in 5f is based on the structural assumptions outlined in Chapter Two. In the case of negation in Habitual Aspect, the Present Tense marker is optionally dropped, as the example in 5b shows.[4] However, this is not true in the case of the Past Tense, as illustrated in 5c.

3.2.2 Negation in Progressive Aspect

The Progressive Aspect marker in Hindi is *rah*. It occurs to the right of the verb stem. Number and Gender morphemes occur to the right of the Progressive Aspect marker at the edge of the verbal unit. As far as the interaction of the Progressive Aspect marker and negation is concerned, the negative marker may precede the entire verbal complex or, in the case of sentential negation, follow the entire verbal complex, as shown in 6b and 6c. In the case of Progressive Aspect, the verbal morphology is not as complex as it is in the case of Habitual Aspect. The example in 6a is an affirmative counterpart of 6b. There is no strict adjacency requirement between the verb stem and the Progressive Aspect marker, because the Progressive Aspect marker is an independent word. Therefore, elements such as negative markers can intervene between the verb and the Progressive marker.

(6) a. maiN   skuul   jaa rahaa   huuN/thaa
          I   school   go   PROG-MASC   am/was
          'I am/was going to school.'

      b. maiN   skuul   nahiiN jaa   rahaa   huuN/thaa
          I   school   NEG   go   PROG-MASC   am/was
          'I am/was not going to school.'

      c. maiN   skuul   jaa nahiiN rahaa   huuN/thaa
          I   school   go   NEG   PROG-MASC   am/was
          'I am/was not going to school.'

      d.

Once again, I give the representation in 6d to make clear the structural assumptions (outlined in Chapter Two) regarding the placement of the Progressive Aspect marker. It seems very intuitive that in Hindi the Progressive Aspect marker comes from the verb *rahnaa* 'to stay.' The occurrence of the Progressive Aspect maker as an independent word, unlike the occurrence of the Habitual Aspect marker as a clitic, is very crucial for understanding the order of constituents in the clause structure of Hindi. It becomes really very significant for locating the negation phrase in Hindi clause structure, which is discussed later in this chapter.

3.2.3 Negation in Perfective Aspect

The Perfective Aspect marker in Hindi is–*aa*. This occurs on the verb stem to
the right. The Number and Gender morphemes are also realized at the right
edge of the verbal complex. It is important to mention here that the Perfective
Aspect marker is homophonous with the Gender agreement markers; as in most
of the verbs, there appears to be only the agreement (Gender and Number)
markers on the verb in the Perfective Aspect. As far as the interaction of the Perfective Aspect marker and negation is concerned, the negative marker precedes
the entire verbal complex in the case of sentential negation, as in 7b, which is a
negative counterpart of 7a, and follows the entire verbal complex in the case of
constituent negation, as in 7c. Since the verbal morphology is a complex of several clitics, there is a strict adjacency requirement between them. Strict adjacency is maintained between the Perfective Aspect marker and the agreement
marker, as the ungrammaticality of the example in 7d shows.

(7)   a.   raajiiv   skuul   ga-yaa
           rajiv   school   go-PERF
           'Rajiv went to school.'

      b.   raajiiv   skuul   nahiiN   ga-yaa
           rajiv   school   NEG   go-PERF
           'Rajiv did not go to school.'

      c.   raajiiv   skuul   ga-yaa   nahiiN
           rajiv   school   go-PERF   NEG
           'Rajiv did no go to school.'

      d. * raajiiv   skuul   gay- nahiiN-aa
           rajiv   school   go-NEG-PERF
           'Rajiv did not go to school.'

      e.

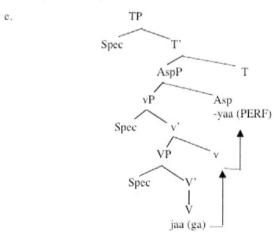

The representation in 7e shows the structural assumptions in the above discussion of Perfective Aspect in Hindi clause structure.

3.3 Negation in Imperative Mood

In this section, I discuss negation in Imperatives. There are three forms of
second person pronouns in Hindi. They are *aap* (formal), *tum* (informal),
and *tuu* (very informal). Since the verb morphology illustrates the three-
way distinction, the presence of the pronoun in a sentence is optional.
There are two other forms of Imperative Mood in Hindi. They are the
infinitival Imperative and the Future Imperative. The infinitival Imperative is also known as the neutral Imperative, as its subject can be any one
of the three different forms of the second person pronoun. On the other
hand, the Future Imperative is a more formal type of Imperative than the
formal Imperative, as in 8a. Examples of infinitival and Future Imperatives are given in 8d and 8e, respectively. The optional presence of pronouns and the Imperative verb morphology is illustrated in the following
affirmative sentences:

(8) a. (aap)   ghar   jaa-iye
         you   home   go-IMP-formal
         'Please go home.'

     b. (tum)   ghar   jaa-o
         you   home   go-IMP-informal
         '(Please) go home.'

     c. (tuu)   ghar   jaa
         you   home   go-IMP-very informal
         'Go home.'

     d. (tuu/tum/aap) ghar   jaa-naa
         you   home   go-IMP-INF-neutral
         'Go home.'

     e. (aap)   ghar   jaa-iyegaa
         you   home   go-IMP-FUT
         'Please go home.'

The representation in 8f shows the placement of the Imperative in the clause
structure of Hindi. The Imperative marker is in the head position of the
Mood phrase (MoodP).

    Negative markers precede imperative verbs, as shown in the following
examples:

f.

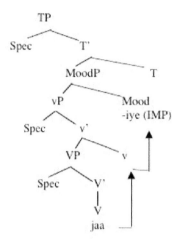

(9) a. (aap)   ghar   mat/nahiiN/na jaa-iye
       you   home   NEG   go-IMP-formal
       Please do not go home.'

   b. (tum)   ghar   mat/nahiiN/na jaa-o
       you   home   NEG   go-IMP-informal
       '(Please) don't go home.'

   c. (tuu)   ghar   mat/nahiiN/na jaa
       you   home   NEG   go-IMP-very informal
       'Don't go home.'

   d. (tuu/tum/aap) ghar   mat/nahiiN/na jaa-naa
       you   home   NEG   go-IMP-INF-neutral
       'Don't go home.'

   e. (aap)   ghar   mat/nahiiN/na jaa-iyegaa
       you   home   NEG   go-IMP-FUT
       Don't go home.'

The other aspect of negation in the context of Imperative verbs is the use of the alternative negative marker *mat*.[5] It is worth mentioning here that this negative marker occurs mostly in the context of Imperatives and sometimes in Subjunctives. The other two negative markers do occur in the Imperative sentence as well, as shown in 9, but the negative marker *mat* does not occur in any non-Imperative (Mood) context, as shown in 10.

(10) a. maiN   maNdir   nahiiN   jaa-taa
       I   temple   NEG   go-HAB-MASC-SG
       'I do not go to temple.'

   b. *maiN   maNdir   mat   jaa-taa
       I   temple   NEG   go-HAB-MASC-SG
       'I do not go to temple.'

3.4 Negation in Subjunctive Mood

In this section, I discuss the presence of negative markers in the context of
the Subjunctive Mood. As discussed in Chapter Two, the Subjunctive Mood
in Hindi is also marked by a clitic on the verb, which does not carry any
Gender information. The following examples illustrate this fact:

(11) a. maiN   ghar   jaa-uN
       I   home   go-SUBJ
       'May I go home?'

   b. vah   ghar   jaa-ye
       he   home   go-SUBJ
       'He may go home.'

   c. aap   ab   ghar   jaa-yeN
       you   now   home   go-SUBJ
       'You may go home now.'

   d. ve   ab   ghar   jaa-yeN
       they   now   home   go-SUBJ
       'They may go home now.'

(12) aap   mere   ghar   aayeN   to   mujhe   khushii   ho-gii
     you   my   house   come-SUBJ then   to me   happiness happen-FUT
     'I will be happy if you come to my place.'

(13) a. bhagwaan   aap   ko   lambii   umra   de-N
        god   you   to   long   life   give-SUBJ
        'May god give you long life!'

In the examples mentioned above, I show that the Subjunctive marker is a
clitic on the verb, as is clear from the morphology of the verb. The subjunctive marker carries Number and Person agreement.

The following structure, in 13b, shows the placement of Subjunctive
Mood in the clause structure of Hindi. Just like the Imperative Mood, the
Subjunctive Mood too is in the head position of the Mood phrase.

13b.

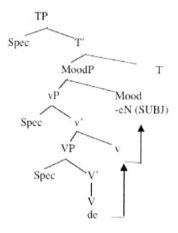

With regard to structural assumptions (illustrated in Chapter Two), I will briefly discuss here the phrasal hierarchy between between MoodP and AspP. The MoodP precedes the AspP, as the example in 13c shows, and then dictates the structural representation in 13d. (13c is an example of Presumptive Mood.) As discussed in Chapter Two, the verb moves to the v and then v moves to Asp. The order of the morphemes on the verb shows that the Modal morpheme follows the Aspectual morpheme. This suggests that the v+Asp moves to the Mood (the head of the MoodP). Finally, this suggests that the MoodP figures higher than the AspP in clause structure.

(13) c. yadii   aap   aa   rahe   ho-N   to ...
        if   you   come   PROG   PRESUM   then
        'If you are coming then . . . '

d.

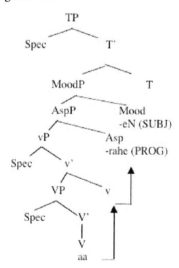

Now I turn to the negative Subjunctive. Let us consider the following examples:

(14) a. maiN ghar na jaa-uN
   I   home NEG go-SUBJ
   'May I not go home?'

  b. vah ghar na jaa-ye
   he   home NEG go-SUBJ
   'He may not go home.'

  c. aap ghar na jaa-yeN
   you home NEG go-SUBJ
   'You may not go home now.'

  d. ve ab ghar na jaa-yeN
   they now home NEG go-SUBJ
   'They may not go home now.'

(15) a. dhumrapaan na kar-eN
   smoking   NEG do-SUBJ
   'Please do not smoke!'

  b. ? dhumrapaan mat kar-eN
    smoking   NEG do-SUBJ
    'Please do not smoke!'

  c. ? dhumrapaan nahiiN kar-eN
    smoking   NEG do-SUBJ
    'Please do not smoke!'

The negative marker *na* precedes the Subjunctive verbs in Hindi. The other marker of negation, *nahiiN*, may also occur in the context, as shown above in 15c; however, *na* is the preferred choice, as shown in 15a. On the other hand, the Imperative negative *mat* does not appear to be a preferred choice, as shown in 15b.

3.5 Negation and Modal Verbs

In this section, I discuss the distribution of negation in the context of the five Modal verbs in Hindi: *saknaa, paanaa, cuknaa, paRnaa,* and *caahiye.* A description of the formation of Modal verbs is discussed in Chapter Two. Similar to other Modals, they do not occur independently in a sentence with a Modal meaning; they require the support of the main verb.

(16) a. raajiiv   cal   sak-taa   hai
         rajiv   walk   MOD-HAB   is
         'Rajiv can walk.'

     b. maiN   mushkil se   khaa   paa-yaa
         I   hardly   eat   MOD-PERF
         'I could hardly eat.'

     c. maiN   khaa   cukaa   thaa
         I   eat   MOD-PERF   was
         'I had already eaten.'

     d. mujhe   ghar   jaa-naa   paRaa
         I   home   go-INF   MOD-PERF
         'I had to go home.'

     e. mujhe   ghar   jaa-naa   caahiye
         I   home   go-INF   mod
         'I should go home.'

     f. mujhe   ghar   jaa-naa   ho-gaa
         I   home   go-INF   MOD-FUT
         'I will have to go home.'

The examples given above show the distribution of modal verbs in affirmative sentences. The modal verb *saknaa* 'can' indicates the capability of the agent to do a certain action. The modal verb *paanaa* is also a capability marker. The modal *cuknaa* indicates completion, whereas *paRnaa* marks compulsion. It is worth mentioning that the modal verb *paRnaa* is different from the rest of the modals in that in the case of *paRnaa* the main verb occurs in infinitival form, as shown in 16d. Similarly, the example in 16e shows that the Modal verb *caahiye* 'should' takes an infinitival complement; also it does not agree with the agent.

The distribution of negative markers with Modal verbs is interesting from the point of view of the position of negation in the Hindi clause structure. There are two positions in which negative markers may occur in the context of Modal verbs to denote sentential negation. The negative marker can either precede the entire verbal complex, as shown in 17b, or it can follow the stem of the main verb and precede the Modal, as shown in 17a. It is never the case that a negative marker follows the entire verbal complex, except in constituent negation. Consider the following examples:

(17) a. raajiiv cal nahiiN sak-taa
   rajiv walk NEG MOD-HAB
   'Rajiv cannot walk.'

 b. raajiiv nahiiN cal sak-taa
   rajiv NEG walk MOD-HAB
   'Rajiv cannot walk.'

 c. main nahiiN khaa paa-yaa
   I NEG eat MOD-PERF
   'I could not eat.'

 d. maiN khaa nahiiN paa-yaa
   I eat NEG MOD-PERF
   'I could not eat.'

 e. ? maiN nahiiN khaa cuk-aa thaa
   I NEG eat MOD-PERF was
   'I had not already eaten.'

 f. ? maiN khaa nahiiN cuk-aa thaa
   I eat NEG MOD-PERF was
   'I had not already eaten.'

 g. mujhe ghar nahiiN jaa-naa paR-aa
   I home NEG go-INF MOD-PERF
   'I did not have to go home.'

 h. mujhe ghar jaa-naa nahiiN paR-aa
   I home go-INF NEG MOD-PERF
   'I did not have to go home.'

 i. mujhe ghar nahiiN jaa-naa caahiye
   I home NEG go-INF MOD
   'I should not go home.'

 j. mujhe ghar jaanaa nahiiN caahiye
   I home go-INF NEG MOD
   'I should not go home.'

As illustrated in the examples above, sentential negatives can in Hindi precede as well as follow the main verb in the presence of a Modal verb. Also, the preferred negative marker in a structure using a Modal is *nahiin*. It is also an interesting point that the presence of the negative with the Modal verb *cuknaa* is slightly odd. At this point, I do not have an explanation for this irregularity.

  Modal verbs are very similar to the aspectual verb constructions also known as compound verbs or serial verb constructions in Hindi.[6] Compound

verbs are a sequence of two verbs where the first one is called "explicator" or
"null" and the second verb carries all the agreement morphology (Kachru 1965,
Hook 1974, Shapiro 1974, and van Olphen 1970). Such a construction is similar to Modal verbs only to the extent that Modal verbs are also serial verbs;
however, modal verbs are remarkably different from compound verbs of Hindi
for semantic reasons. Another difference between Modal verbs and compound
verbs lies in the fact that a serial verb construction of an infinitival verb and a
Modal verb can be negated as shown above; however, aspectual verbs or compound verbs cannot be negated, as shown in the following examples:

(18) a. raajiiv   ko   aa-naa   nahiiN   paR-aa
         rajiv   to   come   NEG   MOD-PERF
         'Rajiv did not have to come.'

     b. raajiiv-ne   ghar   bec   diy-aa
         rajiv-ERG   house   sell   give-PERF
         'Rajiv sold his house.'

     c. * raajiiv-ne   ghar   nahiiN   bec   diy-aa
          rajiv-ERG   house   NEG   sell   give-PERF
          'Rajiv did not sell his house.'

     d. ?/* raajiiv-ne   ghar   bec   nahiiN   diy-aa
            rajiv-ERG   house   sell   NEG   give-PERF
            'Rajiv did not sell his house.'

In 18a, a Modal verb is being negated, whereas in 18c and 18d, an
aspectual verb is being negated. It is not possible, as shown in 18c, to negate
a serial or compound verb construction, it is also unacceptable with the sentential negative interpretation, as shown in 18d. However, 18d is grammatical with a question interpretation. This question interpretation is also
different in the sense that these questions carry a sense of affirmation.

Gaeffke (1968) and Hook (1974) show several such cases and argue
that aspectual verbs can be negated in Hindi. The examples in Gaeffke
clearly show that compound verbs or serial verbs can only be negated with
sentential negative interpretation in the case of the Future Imperative and
Subjunctive Moods, as in 19.

(19) a. aap   mujhe   bhuul   na   jaa-iyegaa
         you   I-DAT   forget   NEG   go-IMP-FUT
         'Don't forget me.'

     b. raajiiv   kahiiN   galatii   na   kar   baiTh-e
         rajiv   in case   mistake   NEG   do   sit-SUBJ
         'Hope Rajiv does not make a mistake.'

The example in 19a is in the Future Imperative Mood, whereas the example in 19b is in the Subjunctive Mood. Both examples contain compound verbs, such as *bhuul jaana* 'forget' and *kar baiThnaa* 'do.' They are negated with the sentential negative interpretation. However, these too express doubt, just as the negated aspectual verbs are in other aspects questions with affirmative interpretations and express doubt. Thus, it is clear that compound verbs or serials verbs cannot be negated in Hindi and retain the same semantic interpretation.

3.6 Negation and Light Verbs

In this section, I discuss the distribution of negative markers in the context of light verbs in Hindi. We have seen that negative markers occur in a different position in the context of Modal verbs. Similar to the occurrence of negation in the context of Modals, negation markers in the context of light verbs can either precede the entire verbal complex (i.e. NEG +N-/Adj+V) or precede only the verb (i.e. N-/Aadj+NEG+V).

The presence of negative markers in the case of light verbs relates crucially to the issue of the projection of negation in Hindi clause structure. First, let us have a brief look at the light verbs in Hindi. There are two types of light verbs in Hindi. They have either N-V or Adj-V sequence. The verb forms are either *honaa* 'to be' or *karnaa* 'to do' (Shapiro 1974, Hook 1974, Abbi 1994). A large number of light verbs consist of a noun or an adjective followed by *karnaa,* for example: *samaapt karnaa* 'to talk,' *kaam karnaa* 'to work,' *saaf karnaa* 'to clean,' *and acchaa lagnaa* 'to seem/feel good.'

(20) a. maiN-ne apnaa kaam samaapt kiy-aa
     I-ERG self work finish do-PERF
     'I finished my work.'

   b. pulis-ne apnaa kaam kiy-aa
     police-ERG self work do-PERF
     'Police did its job.'

   c. raajiiv sariitaa se shaadi kar-egaa
     rajiv sarita with marriage do-FUT
     'Rajiv will marry Sarita.'

The nouns and adjectives that appear in light verbs with *karnaa* usually also appear with *honaa,* such as *samaapt honaa* 'to be finished,' *khatam honaa* 'to be done,' *saaf honaa* 'to be cleaned,' *acchaa honaa* 'to be good,' *buraa honaa* 'to be bad.'

(21) a. meraa   kaam   samaapt   huaa
         my   work   finish   happen-PERF
         'My work is done.'

     b. aapkaa   kaam   khatam   huaa
         your   work   finish   happen-PERF
         'Did you get your job done?'

     c. kal   sariitaa ke   bahan   kii   shaadii   huii
         yesterday sarita   of   sister of   wedding   happen-PERF
         'Sarita's sister got married yesterday.'

Light verbs consisting of a noun or adjective with *karnaa* and light verbs with the same noun and adjective followed by *honaa* are syntactically related: the light verbs with *karnaa* are transitive, whereas the light verbs with *honaa* are intransitive.

I will briefly elaborate on the structural assumptions of light verbs in the clause structure of Hindi. The following representation, in 21d, displays the position of light verbs in Hindi clause structure.

(21) d.

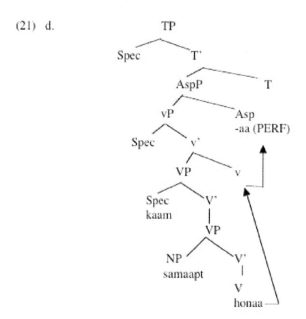

Now I turn to the distribution of negative markers with light verbs. Negative markers may precede the entire light verb complex (i.e. the nominal or the adjectival part and the verb). In addition, a negative marker may occur following the nominal or the adjectival part of the light verb and precede the verb. In either case, the negative markers do not follow the entire light verb complex. The following examples illustrate this.

(22) a. maiN-ne   kaam   nahiiN   shuru   kiy-aa
      I-ERG   work   NEG   begin   do-PERF
      'I did not start working.'

   b. maiN-ne   kaam   shuru   nahiiN   kiy-aa
      I-ERG   work   begin   NEG   do-PERF
      'I did not start working.'

   c. meraa   kaam   nahiiN   samaapt   huaa
      my   work   NEG   finish
      'My work is not done.'

   d. meraa   kaam   samaapt   nahiiN   huaa
      my   work   finish   NEG   happen-PERF
      'My work is not done.'

The examples in 22b and 22d show that the negative marker *nahiiN* can occur between the noun and the light verb sequence; but it may also precede the whole sequence, as in 22a and 22c, and intercept the adjacency between the nominal or adjectival component and the verbal component of the light verb sequence. However, the negation marker cannot follow the entire N-/Adj-V sequence of the light verb in the sense of sentential negation.

4. POSITION OF NEGATION IN HINDI SENTENCES

In this chapter, I have so far shown the distribution of negative markers in sentences in general and their interaction with the different components of a sentence, namely tense, aspect, and modality. In the following subsections of this chapter, I will discuss the implications of the occurrence of negative markers in different positions in the Hindi sentence.

There are several positions in a sentence where a negative marker can occur. It has been suggested, in studies such as Bhatia (1978), that the immediately pre-verbal position is associated with sentential negation. A negative marker in any other position marks constituent negation. I will discuss both sentential negation and constituent negation here and present evidence that the negation immediately preceding the verb is in fact the sentential negation.

4.1 Pre-verbal (Sentential) Negation

The occurrence of negative elements in the pre-verbal position marks sentential negation in the unmarked word order in Hindi, as discussed in Bhatia (1978) and shown in the data in example 23. Later in this chapter I present several pieces of evidence in support of pre-verbal negation as the marker of sentential negation in Hindi and in the syntactic representation of sentential negation.

(23) a. maiN   aam   nahiiN   khaa-taa
       I   mango NEG   eat-HAB
       'I do not eat mango.'

    b. aap   kaheN   to   maiN   na   jaa-uN
       you   say-SUBJ   then   I   NEG   go-SUBJ
       'If you say then I may not go.'

    c. aap   mat   jaa-iye
       you   NEG   go-IMP
       'Please do not go.'

In 23, above, we observe that all the negative markers are in the immediately pre-verbal position. A negative marker in such a position takes scope over the entire sentence. For example, the sentence in 23a means 'I do not eat mango' and not 'It is not mango that I eat, but I eat something else.'

4.2 Constituent Negation

In the Hindi sentence, a negative marker may also occur in a position other than the immediately pre-verbal. Such a phenomenon, when the negative marker does not immediately precede the verb, is called constituent negation and is shown in example 24. In the case of constituent negation, the negative markers immediately follow the constituents they negate. This description of constituent negation is based on both the linear order of the negation marker and other constituents in a sentence, as well as the interpretation of a sentence. The negated constituent and negative marker are illustrated in italics in the following examples:

(24) a. maiN   *aam*   *nahiiN*   khaa-taa
       I   mango NEG   eat-HAB
       'I do not eat mango.'
       'I do not eat mango, but I eat something else.'

    b. maiN   aam   *khaa-taa*   *nahiiN*
       I   mango eat-HAB   NEG
       'I do not eat mango.'
       'I do not eat mango, but I sell mango.'

    c. *maiN*   *nahiiN*   aam   khaa-taa
       I   NEG   mango   eat-HAB
       'I do not eat mango.'
       'I do not eat mango, but someone else may eat mango.'

In 24a, the negation marker is in the pre-verbal position; however, if it is associated with the object *aam* 'mango,' then it negates only the object NP and does not remain a sentential negative anymore. In 24b, the negation marker follows the verb, and in this position the negation marker negates only the verb. In 24c, the negation marker follows the subject NP, and it negates only the subject NP. We notice from the data in 24 that constituent negation in Hindi is XP-final (i.e. XP-*nahiiN*), while sentential negation seems to precede the verb only. I will discuss the representation of sentential negation and constituent negation in Hindi clause structure in the next section.

To summarize this section, if a negative marker is in the immediately pre-verbal position, it expresses sentential negation, while in other positions negation markers indicate constituent negation. In the case of sentential negation, the entire sentence is in the scope of the negative, whereas in the case of constituent negation only a particular constituent (what is followed by the negative) is in the scope of the negative.

4.3 Evidence for Immediately Pre-verbal Position as Sentential Negation

As discussed above, negative markers in the immediately pre-verbal position express sentential negation, and in other positions they indicate constituent negation. The question that arises is, How do we know that negative markers in the pre-verbal position are sentential negatives? The evidence in support of pre-verbal negation as a sentential negative comes from the interaction of light verbs and negation and from the interaction between modal verbs and negation. There are two positions (N-/Adj-NEG-V and NEG-N-/Adj-V), in which negation markers occur in the context of light verbs and Modals. Let us have a look at the examples in 25.

(25) N-/Adj-NEG-Verb

    a. maiN-ne apnaa   kaam   samaapt nahiiN ki-yaa
       I-ERG   self   work   finish   NEG   do-PERF
       'I did not finish my work.'

    NEG-N-/Adj-Verb

    b. maiN-ne apnaa   kaam   nahiiN samaapt ki-yaa
       I-ERG   self   work   NEG   finish   do-PERF
       'I did not finish my work.'

    Verb-NEG-Modal

    c. maiN   khaa   nahiiN   sak-aa
       I   eat   NEG   MOD-PERF
       'I did not finish my work.'

NEG-Verb-Modal

d. maiN   nahiiN   khaa   sak-aa
   I   NEG   eat   MOD-PERF
   'I did not finish my work.'

My claim is that irrespective of the order of constituents in the verbal complex in the above examples (NEG-N-/Adj-V or N-/Adj-NEG-V), the negative element is the marker of sentential negation. I provide two pieces of evidence below to show that the positioning of negative elements in either order in conjunct verbs and Modals are evidence of sentential negation.

It has been argued that only sentential negation licenses NPIs (Bhatia 1978, Mahajan 1990a, and Benmamoun 1997, among others). Let us consider the examples in 26a and 26b and 26d and 26e. The NPI *kisii bhii* is licensed by the presence of the negative marker in each sentence. In every case, negative marker is the sentential negative that licenses the NPI. On the other hand, constituent negation does not license the NPI, as shown in 26c and 26f. The examples in 26c and 26f are ungrammatical in the intended reading of the element *kisii bhii* 'anyone' as an NPI; otherwise 26c and 26f are well formed in indefinite readings.

(26) a. raajiiv   kisii   se   bhii   shaadii   nahiiN   [$_V$ kar-egaa]
        raajiiv   anyone   with   EMPH   marriage   NEG   do-FUT
        'Rajiv will not marry anyone.'

     b. raajiiv   kisii   se   bhii   nahiiN   [$_V$ shaadii   kar-egaa]
        raajiiv   anyone   with   EMPH   NEG   marriage   do-FUT
        'Rajiv will not marry anyone.'

     c. * [raajiiv   nahiiN]   kisii   se   bhii   shaadii   [$_V$ kar-egaa]
          raajiiv   NEG   anyone   with   EMPH   marriage   do-FUT
          'Not Rajiv will marry anyone.'

     d. maiN   kisii   ko   bhii   nahiiN   dekh   sak-aa
        I   anyone   to   EMPH   NEG   see   MOD-PERF
        'I could not see anyone.'

     e. maiN   kisii   ko   bhii   dekh   nahiiN   sak-aa
        I   anyone   to   EMPH   see   NEG   MOD-PERF
        'I could not see anyone.'

     f. */? maiN   nahiiN   kisii   ko   bhii   dekh   sak-aa
        I   NEG   anyone   to   EMPH   see   MOD-PERF
        'I could not see anyone.'

The second piece of evidence showing that the negative elements in light verbs are sentential negatives is as follows: it has also been argued that only the sentential negative has scope over quantifiers, as illustrated in 27. The reading of 27a and 27b is ambiguous. Both sentences have two readings. The first reading is that Sarita does not make friends with everybody in general; she makes friends with a selective type of people. The second reading is that Sarita does not want to make friends with a particular person. The first reading is the preferred one. The sentence is not ambiguous, however, in the presence of the constituent negation, as in 27c, which has only one reading: others may make friends with everybody, but Sarita is definitely not the one who will do so.

(27) a. sariitaa   sab   se   dostii   nahiiN   kar-tii   [ambiguous]
        sarita   all   with   friendship   NEG   do-HAB
        'Sarita does not make friends with everybody (in general).'
        'Sarita does not make friends with everybody (keeping one person in mind).'

     b. sariitaa   sab   se   nahiiN   dostii   kar-tii   [ambiguous]
        sarita   all   with   NEG   friendship   do-HAB
        'Sarita does not make friends with everybody (in general).'
        'Sarita does not make friends with everybody (keeping one person in mind).'

     c. sariitaa   nahiiN   sab   se   dostii   kar-tii   [unambiguous]
        sarita   NEG   all   with   friendship   do-HAB
        'It is not Sarita who makes friends with everybody.'

Thus, on the basis of the data presented regarding the licensing of negative polarity items and scope over quantifiers, I conclude that immediately pre-verbal negation can be interpreted as sentential negation in Hindi.

5. REPRESENTATION OF NEGATION IN HINDI CLAUSE STRUCTURE

Thus far in this chapter we have seen the distribution of negation in Hindi sentences. We have seen the differences between constituent negation and sentential negation, along with evidence from the interaction of conjunct verbs and modal verbs for the immediately pre-verbal negation marker as sentential negation. The next question that arises is how negative markers are syntactically represented.

In this section, I will first discuss the position of negation in the clause structure of UG as proposed by Pollock (1989) and Chomsky (1989 and 1995). I will also discuss Zanuttini's (1991) proposal for the placement of

negation in the clause structure of some of the Romance languages. I will
then discuss the proposal for the position of negation in Hindi clause structure in Mahajan (1990a); and finally I will present my proposal for the location of sentential negation in Hindi clause structure. Before I conclude this
chapter, I will also discuss the representation of constituent negation in the
clause structure and some of the contexts of negation that do not contain
negation markers.

5.1 Negation in the Clause Structure of UG

The structure in 28 gives the representation of negation in the clause structure. Following Pollock (1989), Chomsky (1989) treats negation as a phrasal
category where negation heads its own maximal projection and occurs in the
functional layer of the clause structure below TP. In such a system, NegP
occurs between TP and AgroP, and the position of TP and NegP in the
clause structure figures below AgrsP and AgroP.

(28)

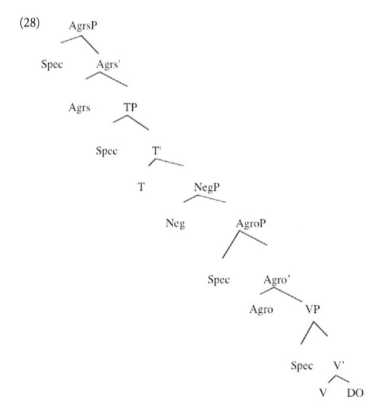

The structure in 28 is similar to the representation of negation in Pollock (1989), shown below. Pollock also shows that negation heads its own maximal projection and occurs in the functional layer of the clause structure below TP. In Pollock's system, NegP occurs between TP and AgrP. In fact, his argument for the split of IP into TP and AgrP is largely based on the position of negation in the clause structure.

(29)

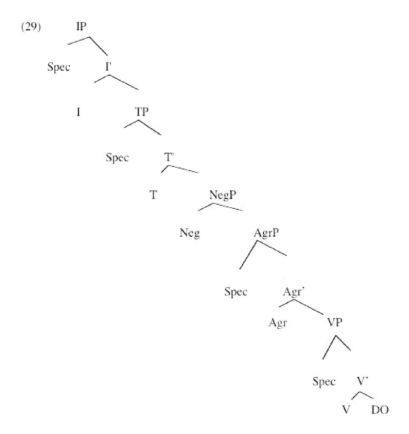

5.2 Representation of Negation in Zanuttini (1991)

Romance languages have two broad classes of negative markers: the pre-verbal negative markers in languages such as Italian, Spanish, Catalan, Portuguese, and Romanian, among others, and the post-verbal negative markers in languages such as Occitan, Valdotain, Piedmontese, and Sursilvan, among others (Zanuttini 1991). These languages employ three basic strategies in

negating a clause. In the first strategy negative markers are in pre-verbal position, whereas in the second strategy the negative markers are in post-verbal
position. Negative markers in post-verbal position always follow the main
verb when the main verb is finite. In the third strategy, pre-verbal and post-
verbal negative markers co-occur.

Pre-verbal negative markers occur in a language as the only negative
constituent if they are located in a structural position that c-commands the
finite verb, as in 30a. If the negative marker is in a position that does not c-
command the finite verb, it cannot occur as the only negative constituent in
the clause, as shown in 30b.

Pre-verbal negative markers:

(30) a. maria   no   se   lo   dio   (Spanish)
        Maria   NEG   him   it   give-PERF
        'Maria did not give it to him.'

    b. * he   visto   a   nadie   (Spanish)
         have   seen   to   no one
         'I have seen no one.'

The examples in 31a illustrate post-verbal negation markers in
Romance languages such as Italian, Spanish, and Portuguese. In these languages a post-verbal negative marker does not occur in the absence of a pre-
verbal negative marker, as in 31b.

Post verbal negation markers:

(31) a. *non* ho visto *nessuno* (Italian)
        no he visto a *nadie* (Spanish)
        naNo vi *ninguem* (Portuguese)
        'I haven't seen anybody.'

    b. * ho visto *nessuno* (Italian)
       * he visto a *nadie* (Spanish)
       * vi *ninguem* (Portuguese)
       'I haven't seen anybody.'

The examples in 32 illustrate co-occurrence of pre-verbal and post-verbal negation markers in Romance languages such as Italian, Spanish, and
Portuguese.

Co-occurrence of preverbal as well as post-verbal negative markers:

(32) *nessuno* ha detto *nessuno* (Italian)
    nadie ha dicho *nada* (Spanish)
    ninguem (*naNo*) disse *nada* (Portuguese)
    'Nobody has said anything.'

The two NegPs are called NegP1 and NegP2. According to Zanuttini (1991), NEG is not consistently located in the head position of the NegP in these languages. Consider the following structure:

(33)

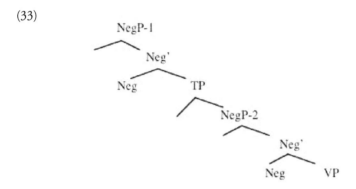

    NegP1 has strong features in the languages that have pre-verbal negative constituents and weak features in the languages that have post-verbal negative constituents. A strong feature does not need to be checked in syntax, whereas a weak feature needs to be checked by movement at LF. Therefore, in a language with a strong feature in NegP1, a negative clause must have a negative marker in NegP1, or a negative element in a position c-commanding NegP1. If a negative constituent or an element is not present in NegP1, ungrammaticality will ensue, as the strong feature of a functional projection (NegP1) is not checked in syntax. In languages containing a weak feature in NegP1, a negative clause need not have a negative constituent in NegP1 or a negative element in a position c-commanding NegP1 in syntax. Rather, negative constituents or negative elements in structurally lower positions can rise at LF and check the weak feature of NegP1.

    The claim is that NegP1 is a position where the syntactic feature corresponding to sentential negation can be found, as negative elements in NegP1 c-command the verb. Having discussed the representation of negation in languages other than Hindi, I will now consider the representation of negation in the clause structure of Hindi as found in Mahajan (1990a) and Dwivedi (1991).

5.3 Representation of Negation in Mahajan (1990a) and Dwivedi (1991)

Mahajan (1990a) suggests that in Hindi, negation heads its own maximal projection NegP and occurs below TP. Mahajan adopts the structure proposed by Chomsky (1989) for the clause structure of Hindi. However, on the basis of DO scrambling, Mahajan argues that the displacement of negation at LF is required for independent reasons in Hindi. According to Mahajan, such an assumption is independent of the licensing of negative polarity items. In the next chapter, I suggest that the displacement of negation at LF is not a requirement in Hindi. The following tree shows the representation of negation in Mahajan for Hindi clause structure:

(34)

```
            AgrsP
           /\
      Spec    Agrs'
             /\
         Agrs    TP
                /\
            Spec   T'
                  /\
                 T    NegP
                     /\
                 Spec    Neg'
                        /\
                      Neg   AgroP
```

Dwivedi (1991) also suggests that negation in Hindi heads its own phrase, NegP. She argues that despite the fact that negation has traditionally been argued to be a modifier, its distinct syntactic behavior shows that negation is unlike modifiers (determiners, adjectives, adverbs, and quantifiers) in Hindi. While modifiers are syntactically adjuncts, as they are adjoined to the phrases they modify, negation is a head that takes a complement.

According to Dwivedi, constituent negation has its sister (the element that it constituent-negates) to the left in Hindi; hence, negation should be analyzed as an X^0 category. Negation contrasts with other modifiers, such as quantifiers and adjectives, which modify constituents to their right. Let us consider the following example, in 35a, and structure, in 35b:

(35) a. baccoN-ne   [kai   [kaalii   ciRioN   ko]]   caaval   di-yaa
         children-ERG   many   black   birds   to   rice   give-PERF
         'Children gave rice to many black birds.'   (Dwivedi 1991)

  b.

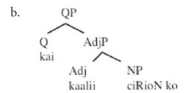

The structure in 35b clearly shows that the quantifier *kai* 'many' and adjective *kaalii* 'black' modify their complements, AdjP (*kaalii ciRioN ko* 'to the black birds') and NP (*ciRioN ko* 'to the birds'), respectively, to the right.

In contrast, negation takes an NP to its left as complement. Consider the following example, in 36a, and representation, in 36b:

(36) a. baccoN-ne   kaalii ciRioN ko nahiiN laal ciRioN ko caaval di-yaa
         children-ERG black birds   to NEG   red birds   to rice   give-PERF
         'Children gave rice not to the black birds, but to the red birds.' (Dwivedi 1991)

  b.

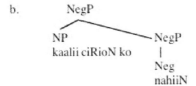

Dwivedi suggests that sentential negation in Hindi selects VP as its complement and occurs in the clause structure below AspP, as shown in 37a and 37b:

(37) a. raam   roTii   nahiiN   khaa-taa   thaa
         raam   bread   NEG   eat-HAB   was
         'Ram did not used to eat bread.'

Dwivedi's suggestion is based purely on the adjacency requirement between the negation and the verb in the case of sentential negation. Thus, Mahajan (1990a) and Dwivedi (1991) agree that NegP occurs below TP in the functional layer. However, Mahajan argues that the NegP obligatorily moves at LF. The difference between the two proposals is minimal.

b.

```
                    TP
                  /    \
              Spec        T'
                        /   \
                   AspP       T
                  /   \      thaa
              NegP      Asp
             /   \      taa
          VP      Neg
         /   \    nahiiN
     Spec     V'
     raam    /  \
          NP     V
        roTii   khaa
```

5.4 Structural Position of Sentential Negation

So far in this section, I have discussed some of the proposals for locating the position of negation in the clause structure of Hindi. Now I will discuss the evidence for the location of negation in the clause structure of Hindi that I proposed in Chapter Two. On the basis of the discussion in this chapter so far and in Chapter Two, it appears that the sentential negative is not inside VP, even though there is an adjacency requirement holding between the sentential negation and the verb; negation appears, rather, to be outside the VP in the functional layer. In order to figure out the position of the sentential negative in the clause structure proposed in the previous chapter, there are two questions that need to be answered: where the negative marker is located in Hindi and what its categorical status is. The answer to both of these questions follows from the discussion thus far. An additional piece of evidence from the following examples in 38:

(38) a. raajiiv   dillii   nahiiN   * (ab)   jaa-yegaa
         rajiv   delhi   NEG   now   go-FUT
         'Now Rajiv will not go to Delhi.'

  b. rajiiv   kaa   dillii   nahiiN   jaa-naa. . . . . .
      rajiv   of   delhi   NEG   go-INF
      'Rajiv's not going to Delhi. . . . . .'   (nominalized clause)

As is clear from the above examples, nothing interrupts the adjacency between the sentential negative and the main verb. I show in (38a) that in the presence of an adverb *ab* 'now' the example in (38a) is ungrammatical. The same sentence is grammatical in the absence of the same adverb. At the same time, even in the case of nominalized clauses, as in 38b, the sentential negative occupies its canonical position. The presence of a time adverb, interrupting the adjacency between the main verb and the sentential negative, results in ungrammaticality. This clearly shows that the negative is not in the Spec position of another phrase, but rather heads its own projection. I propose, therefore, that the syntactic status of the sentential negative is that of head of a phrase. This conclusion is based on the adjacency requirement between the negation and the verb in simple sentences as well as in nominalized clauses, as shown in 38.

Based on the discussions so far in Chapters Two and Three, let us assume that negation heads a maximal projection NegP, as the head occurs to the right, a feature of verb final languages. The head of the NegP also occurs to the right. The position of sentential negation in Hindi clause structure is in 40, which is the structure for 39a.

(39) a. raajiiv   dillii   nahiiN   jaa-taa   hai
         rajiv   delhi   NEG   go-HAB   is
         'Rajiv does not go to Delhi.'

    b. * raajiiv   dillii   jaa   nahiiN   taa   hai
         rajiv   delhi   go   NEG   HAB   is
         'Rajiv does not go to Delhi.'

(40)

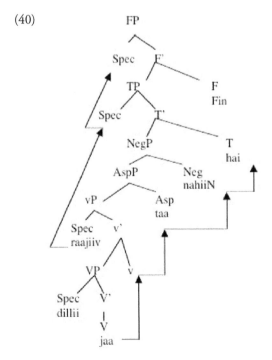

Following Pollock (1989), Chomsky (1989 and 1995), and Mahajan (1990a), I agree that the NegP is located below TP. However, in my proposal the NegP is higher than the AspP. In the above structure, the V moves to v and then to Asp to incorporate the aspectual morpheme. Once it gets the aspectual morphology, this complex (v+Asp) moves to Neg and lands to the right of Neg.[7] From there, the verbal complex plus negation (Neg+verb) moves to T, where it takes the tense morpheme. Regarding the subject, it originates in the Spec of vP. It moves to the Spec of TP for Nominative Case checking, and finally it moves to the Spec of FP for EPP reasons, as discussed in Chapter Two. The sentence thus gets the desired order. Please note that this derivation preserves the adjacency requirement between Neg and the verb. I adopt Dwivedi's (1991) argument that Neg is an X^0 category and heads its own maximal projection, as has been argued in most of the studies on negation, including the ones mentioned above. I differ, however, from Dwivedi in my account of the position of NegP in clause structure. I argue that NegP is higher than AspP and, hence, outside VP. If NegP occurs lower than the AspP, the unacceptability of the sentence in 41b remains unexplained. Let us consider the following sentences:

(41) a. raajiiv   dillii   nahiiN   jaa   rahaa   hai
         rajiv   delhi   NEG   go   PROG   is
         'Rajiv is not going to Delhi.'

      b. ? raajiiv   dillii   jaa   nahiiN   rahaa   hai
           rajiv   delhi   go   NEG   PROG   is
           'Rajiv is not going to Delhi.'

The example in 41b shows that the negation marker *nahiiN* occurs between the verb and the aspect marker. The occurrence of the negation marker between the verb and the aspect marker is possible because the progressive aspect marker *rahaa* is not a morpheme but rather an independent word. It is important to mention here that 41b is not ungrammatical, although it is not the preferred choice. If we assume the NegP to be below the aspect marker, then the example in 41b is predicted to be acceptable. Thus, the unacceptability of 41b, along with the aspectual morphology on the verb, shows that the NegP is located outside the VP and above AspP in the clause structure.

5.4.1 Position of Negation in the Context of Light Verbs

Now that I have established the location of NegP in the clause structure of Hindi, I will look at the derivation of some Hindi sentences to show the position of negation in some of the contexts discussed earlier in this chapter. Recall the discussion of light verb construction in Chapter Two. Light verbs in Hindi are formed by a combination of a noun or an adjective and a verb, mostly *karnaa* 'to do' (transitive) or *honaa* 'to be' (intransitive). The basic mechanism for negation of light verbs is similar to that of simple verbs. Let us consider the examples in 42: the example in 42a is structurally represented in 42b, while the example in 42c is structurally represented in 42d.

(42) a. raajiiv   aufis   saaf nahiiN   kar-taa
        rajiv   office   clean clean   do-HAB
        'Rajiv does not clean the office.'

(42) b.

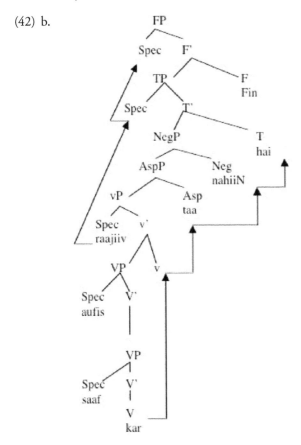

In the first type of light verb N-/Adj-NEG-V, shown in 42a and represented in 42b, the subject *raajiiv* originates at the Spec of vP and moves to the Spec of TP to check Nominative Case; then it further moves to the Spec of FP. On the other hand, the V *kar* 'does' moves to v, and then v moves to the right of Neg for the desirable word order (Neg+v).

Now let us look at the second possibility, Neg-N-/Adj-V, shown in 42c and represented in 42d.

(42) c. raajiiv   aufis   nahiiN   saaf   kar-taa
         rajiv   office   NEG   clean   do-HAB
         'Rajiv does not clean [the?] office.'

(42) d.

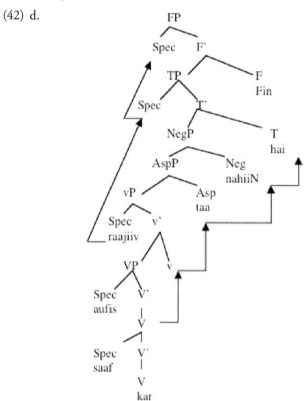

Once again, in the case of the second type of light verbs (Neg-N-/Adj-V), the subject *raajiiv* originates at the Spec of vP and moves to the Spec of TP for Nominative Case and then further moves to the Spec of FP. On the other hand, the V (saaf *kartaa* 'cleans'), which is a compound, moves to v. From there, v further moves to the right of Neg for the desirable word order (Neg-N-/Adj-V).

It has been noted that nouns and verbs usually do not form compounds. However, one of the outcomes of the sequence in 42c is that the N-/Adj-V forms a compound in the presence of a negation marker, as the ungrammaticality of 42e and 42f illustrates.

(42) e. * raajiiv aufis nahiiN kabhii saaf kar-taa hai
        rajiv   office NEG   ever   clean do-HAB-MASC is
        'Rajiv never cleans the office.'

   f. * raajiiv aufis nahiiN saaf kabhii kar-taa hai
        rajiv   office NEG   clean ever   do-HAB-MASC is
        'Rajiv never cleans office.'

The examples in 42e and 42f show that in the presence of a negation marker, no other elements, such as an adverb, may occur between the negation marker and the compound, as in 42e, or between the adjective and the verb, as in 42f.

On account of the strict adjacency requirement between verbs and negative markers, negation appears to be within the VP. However, all the derivations discussed above showing the place of negation in the clause structure of Hindi clearly show that negation is outside the VP. If negation is assumed to be inside the VP, we will have to assume two different structural positions for the negative elements in the clause structure, particularly with reference to light verbs. As discussed above, in the case of light verbs, there seem to be two clearly distinct positions (N-/Adj-Neg-V and Neg-N-/Adj-V) in which sentential negatives can occur. However, that is not the case. Sentential negation in Hindi occurs below TP, and the movement of v derives the correct word order, as shown in the examples above. To conclude the discussion on the structural position of the sentential negative in Hindi clause structure, I have shown, on the basis of the evidence presented above, that Neg heads its own projection and occurs in the functional layer outside the VP, below TP.

5.4.2 Position of Negation in the Context of Mood and Modals

Now I will consider some structures that show the representation of negation in the context of Moods, such as Imperative and Subjunctive, as well as the representation of negation in the context of Modal verbs.

First let us consider the following Imperative, in 43a, and its representation in 43b.

(43) a. (tum) aufis saaf mat kar-o
        you   office clean NEG do-IMP
        'Do not clean the office.'

(43) b.

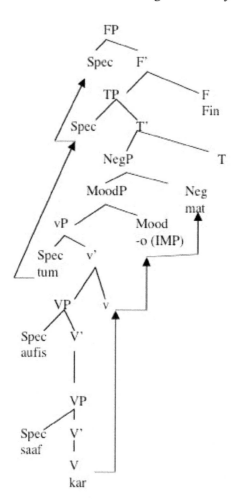

In 43b, the Imperative is in the head of MoodP. In the above structure, the V *kar* 'does' moves to v, and then v moves to Mood. From there, (v+Mood) moves to the right of Neg for the desirable word order (Neg+v).[8]

Now I turn to the representation of negation in Subjunctive Mood. The following example, in 44a, and its representation, in 44b, show negation in the clause structure of Hindi in the context of Subjunctive Mood.

(44) a. aufis   gandaa   na   kar-eN
        office   dirty   NEG   do-SUBJ
        'Do not make the office dirty.'

(44) b.

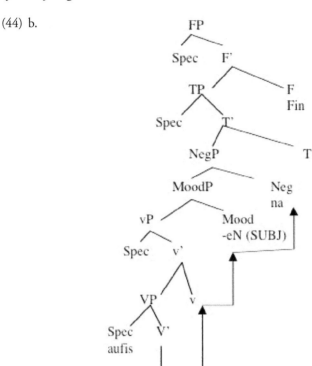

In 44b, which represents 44a, the V *kar* 'does' moves to v, and then v moves to Mood. From there, (v+Mood) moves to the right of Neg for the desirable word order (Neg+v).

In the following two examples, 45 and 46, I give the representation of negation in the context of modals. With the help of such representations, it can also be shown definitively that TP dominates NegP. Consider the following example in 45a and its representation in 45b:

(45) a. tum   aufis   nahiiN   jaa   sak-oge
         you   office   NEG   go   MOD-FUT
         'You will not be able to go to the office.'

(45) b.

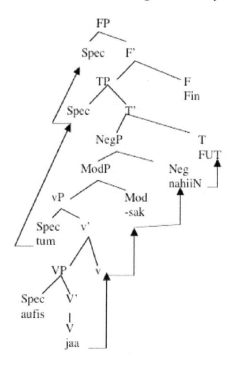

In 45b, the V *jaa* 'go' moves to v, and then v moves to Mod. From there, (v+Mod) moves to the right of Neg. From there, (Neg+v+Mod) moves to T for tense morpheme. Thus, the sentence gets the desirable word order (Neg+v). The structure in 46b shows the representation of negation in the context of modals when they are in the ModP. In 46a, we have both modality and the habitual aspect marker present in the sentence. In such cases, ModP occurs below AspP. This clearly shows that the NegP is directly dominated by TP and dominates AspP, ModP, etc.

(46) a. tum   aufis   nahiiN   jaa   sak-te   ho
        you   office   NEG   go   MOD-HAB   are
        'You cannot go to the office.'

In 46b, the V *jaa* 'go' moves to v, and then v moves to Mod. From there, (v+Mod) moves to AspP for aspectual morpheme, and (v+AspP) lands to the right of Neg for the desirable word order (Neg+v). The further move to T gives the order (Neg+v+T). In the next section, I discuss constituent negation from the point of view of its representation in Hindi clause structure.

(46) b.

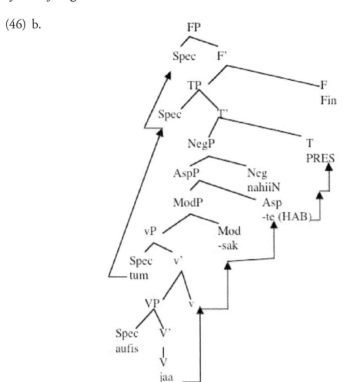

5.5 Structural Position of Constituent Negation

This section discusses the structural positioning of constituent negation. As I have discussed above, the main difference between sentential negation and constituent negation is that the entire sentence is in the scope of sentential negatives, whereas only the constituent that is followed by the negation is in the scope of constituent negatives. As the difference between sentential negation and constituent negation suggests, constituent negation occupies a different position in clause structure. Dwivedi (1991) suggests that constituent negation is also a NegP. I argue that constituent negation is adjoined to the NP or to any other phrase that it takes in its scope. Consider the following examples:

(47) a. raajiiv   aam   nahiiN   khaa-taa
       rajiv   mango   NEG   eat-HAB
       'Rajiv does not eat mango.'
       'Rajiv does not eat mango, [but he eats something else].'

b.

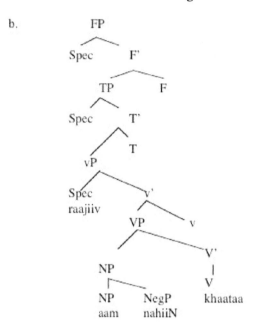

In 47a, the negation marker *nahiiN* negates only the NP *aam* 'mango,' and thus it occupies a different position in the clause structure of Hindi; specifically, it is adjoined to the NP 'mango.' Similarly, in 47c, the negation marker negates only the verb *khaataa* 'eats' and likewise occupies the adjoined position shown in 47d.

(47) c.   maiN   aam   khaa-taa   nahiiN
          I   mango   eat-HAB   NEG
          'I do not eat mango.'
          'I do not eat mango, [but I may do something else with mango].'

d.

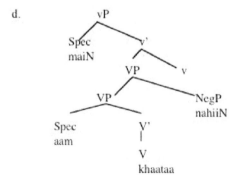

In 47e, negation follows the subject NP, and it negates only the subject *maiN;* 47f shows the position of negation in 47e as adjoined to the subject NP.

(47) e. maiN nahiiN aam   *khaa-taa*
        I   NEG   mango   eat-HAB
    'I do not eat mango.'
    'I do not eat mango, [but someone else may eat mango].'

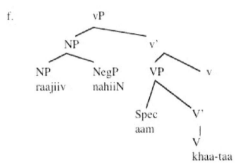

Structures in the above examples show the relative positions of constituent negatives in Hindi sentences. Negatives in all the examples above are adjoined positions: they are adjoined to the phrase that they take in their scope, or that they follow.

Let us consider one more example of constituent negation. In the following example, 48a, there seems to be an interpretation ambiguity. This ambiguity is syntactically resolved. If it is interpreted as a sentential negative, it obviously occupies the position of the sentential negative in the clause structure, as shown above. However, if it is interpreted as a constituent negative, it occurs in an adjoined position, as shown below in 48b.

(48) a. raajiiv raajiiv saaf   nahiiN kar-taa,   gandaa kar-taa   hai
        rajiv   office   clean NEG   do-HAB-MASC dirty   do-HAB-MASC is
    'Rajiv does not clean the office.'
    Lit: 'Rajiv does not clean the office; he makes it dirty. . . . '

The structure in 48b demonstrates the representation of the sentence in 48a with the constituent negation interpretation. If the negative marker in the light verb is interpreted as constituent negation and not as sentential negation, it is adjoined to the adjectival phrase of the light verb.

(48) b.

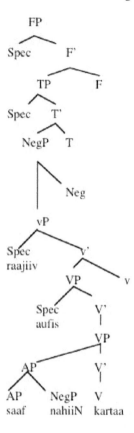

There are certain other ways of expressing negation without a negative marker in Hindi.[9] These do not have any impact syntax; hence, I will not discuss them in this book.

6. CONCLUSION

In this chapter, I presented a detailed description of the distribution of negation in Hindi. I also discussed several related issues, such as the relationship and differences between sentential negation and constituent negation. This chapter explored the structural positions of negation in Hindi clause structure, with particular reference to interactions with light verbs, moods (imperative and subjunctive), and modals. I furthermore elaborated on the different positions possible for negation in clause structure: negation in different tenses, imperative and subjunctive moods, and finally the interaction of negation with light verbs. It is the interaction of light verbs and negative markers that solves the puzzle of the categorical status and location of negatives in the Hindi clause structure. The immediately pre-verbal negation marker is sentential negation, and sentential negation is located outside VP and below TP. Constituent negatives, on the other hand, are located in adjoined positions.

Chapter Four

Negative Polarity Items in Hindi and the Structural Conditions on Their Licensing

1. INTRODUCTION

In the previous chapter, I discussed in detail the location of NegP in the clause structure of Hindi. In this chapter, I will discuss the implications of the location of NegP for the licensing of Negative Polarity Items (NPIs henceforth). This chapter gives a thorough description of NPIs in Hindi and shows the contexts where they are permitted in the presence or absence of a clause mate negation marker (e.g. questions, modality, conditionals, and adversative predicates), then discusses their licensing conditions. On the basis of the occurrence and licensing of NPIs in the presence and absence of a negative licensor, I show that there are clearly two distinct types of NPIs in Hindi: ones that require a clause mate c-commanding negative licensor (strong NPIs) and ones that are permitted in long-distance licensing contexts (weak NPIs). I will discuss previous accounts of Hindi NPI licensing, such as the LF raising of negation proposed by Mahajan (1990a). I will also examine the implications of various proposals for NPI licensing, such as Jackendoff (1969), Lasnik (1975), Ladusaw (1979), Linebarger (1980), Progovac (1994), and Laka (1994). Later in the chapter, I show some problems with the LF based account (Mahajan 1990a) for the licensing of NPIs in Hindi. Finally in this chapter, I outline a proposal for NPI licensing in which I argue that NPIs are licensed overtly and that the licensing of NPIs in Hindi does not involve any covert displacement operation.

2. NEGATIVE POLARITY ITEMS: A DESCRIPTION

In this section, I present a description of NPIs such as *koi bhii*[1] 'any' and *kisii bhii* 'any,' *ek bhii* 'even one,' and *kabhii* 'never,' as well as expressions such as *abhii tak* 'until now,' *ek phuuTii kauRii* 'a red cent,' *Tas se mas na honaa* 'budge an inch,' *baal na baaNkaa karnaa* 'not being able to make a difference,' and *majaal na honaa* 'not being within reach,' which are like NPIs in nature, as they require a negative licensor. I consider them to be NPIs. Both types of NPIs, namely the ones that have traditionally been described as NPIs and the ones that are idiomatic expressions in nature, require negation as their licensor. However, only some of these NPIs (that are not idiomatic expressions) can be permitted in the absence of negative licensors, in contexts such as questions, conditionals, modals, and adversative predicates.

It has been suggested that NPIs are composed of an indefinite and the particle *bhii* 'also/even,' often called an emphatic particle in traditional grammars (Bhatia 1978, Mahajan 1990a, Vasishth 1997 and 1998, Bhandari 1998, and Lahiri 1998). Some of the items that can be combined with *bhii* 'also/even' (in a non-NPI context the emphatic particle *bhii* is equivalent to the English expression *also*) are listed below in 1.

(1) ek 'one'   + bhii 'also/even'   = ek bhii 'even one/any'
     koi 'some'   + bhii 'also/even'   = koi bhii 'any'
     kisii 'some'   + bhii 'also/even'   = kisii bhii 'any'
     kuch 'something'   + bhii 'also/even'   = kuch bhii 'anything'
     kabhii 'sometime'   + bhii 'also/even'   = kabhii bhii 'anytime'

As mentioned above, some other items, which are idiomatic expressions in their common usage, are NPIs. Some of those expressions are listed in 2, below, repeated from the text above.

(2)   a.   *abhii tak* 'so far/until now'
           ek phuuTii kauRii 'a red cent'
           Tas se mas na honaa 'to budge an inch'
           baal na baaNkaa karnaa 'not being able to make a difference'
           majaal na honaa 'not being within reach'

      b.   *koi bhii* 'anybody'
           kisii bhii 'anybody'
           kuch bhii 'anything'

The NPIs listed in 2b do not require negation markers in certain contexts, such as question, modals, conditionals, and adversative predicates.

The following discussion shows the occurrence of NPIs in the presence of a negative licensor.

2.1 NPIs with Clause Mate Negative Licensor

All the NPIs listed in 1 and 2 appear in the presence of a clause mate sentential negation (as discussed in Chapter Three). Consider the following examples:

(3) a. us   kamre meN ek   bhii sTuDeNT nahiiN thaa
           that room   in   one even student   NEG   was
           * 'There wasn't any student in that room.'

      b. * us   kamre meN ek   bhii   sTuDeNT thaa
           that room   in   one even student   was
           * 'There was any student in that room.'

(4) a. us   kamre meN koi bhii   sTuDeNT nahiiN thaa
           that room   in   some even   student   NEG   was
           * 'There was no/not even one (there wasn't any) student in that room.'

      b. * us   kamre meN koi bhii   sTuDeNT thaa
           that room   in   some even   student   was
           * 'There was any student in that room.'

(5) a. maiN-ne kisii bhii   sTuDeNT ko   nahiiN dekh-aa
          I-ERG   some even   student   to   NEG   see-PERF
          'I did not see any student.'

      b. * maiN-ne kisii bhii   sTuDeNT ko   dekh-aa
            I-ERG   some even   student   to   see-PERF
           * 'I saw any student.'

(6) a. maiN-ne kuch   bhii   nahiiN khaa-yaa
          I-ERG   something   even   NEG   eat-PERF
          'I did not eat anything.'

      b. * maiN-ne kuch   bhii   dekh-aa
            I-ERG   something   even   see-PERF
           * 'I saw anything.'

(7) a. maiN kabhii   nahiiN jaa-uNgaa
          I   sometime NEG   go-FUT
          'I will never go.'

      b. * maiN kabhii   jaa-uNgaa
           I   sometime   go-FUT
          'I will never go.'

(8) a. raajiiv   abhii   tak   nahiiN   aa-yaa
         rajiv   now   until   NEG   come-PERF
         'Rajiv has not come so far.'

     b. * raajiiv   abhii   tak   aa-yaa
          rajiv   now   until   come-PERF
          * 'Rajiv has come so far.'

(9) a. maiN   tum   ko   ek   phuuTi   kauRii   nahiiN   du-Ngaa
         I   you   to   one   broken   penny   NEG   give-FUT
         'I will not give you a red cent.'

     b. * maiN   tum   ko   ek   phuuTi   kauRii   du-Ngaa
          I   you   to   one   broken   penny   give-FUT
          * 'I will give you a red cent.'

(10) a. vo   Tas   se mas   nahiiN   huaa
         he   deviate   NEG   happen-PERF
         'He did not budge an inch.'

     b. * vo   Tas   se mas   huaa
          he   deviate   happen-PERF
          * 'He did budge an inch.'

(11) a. raajiiv   tumhaaraa   baal   baaNkaa   nahiiN   kar   sak-egaa
         rajiv   your   hair   disturb   NEG   do   MOD-FUT
         'Rajiv cannot harm you.'

     b. * raajiiv   tumhaaraa   baal   baaNkaa   kar   sak-egaa
          rajiv   your   hair   disturb   do   MOD-FUT
          Rajiv can harm you.'

(12) a. raajiiv   kii   majaal   nahiiN   ki   vo   kuch   bol-egaa
         rajiv   of   possible NEG   that   he   something   speak-FUT
         'It is not possible for Rajiv that he could say something.'

     b. * raajiiv   kii   majaal   ki   vo   kuch   bol-egaa
          rajiv   of   possible that   he   something   speak-FUT
          'It is possible for Rajiv that he could say something.'

NPIs such as *ek bhii* 'even one/any' in 3, *koi bhii* 'any' in 4, *kisii bhii* 'any' in 5, *kuch bhii* 'anything' in 6, *kabhii* 'never' in 7, *abhii tak* 'so far/until now' in 8, *ek phuuTii kauRii* 'a red cent' in 9, *Tas se mas na honaa* 'budge an inch' in 10, *baal na baaNkaa karnaa* 'not being able to make a difference' in 11, and *majaal na honaa* 'not being within reach' in 12 are permitted in the (a) examples, as they are licensed by the negation *nahiiN*. The presence of a negative licensor is obligatory in all the instances above, as shown by the ungrammaticality of all the (b) examples.

There are some other contexts where NPIs can be permitted, even in the absence of a clause mate negation. Some of these contexts are questions, conditionals, modals, adversative predicates, generics, and some cases of imperatives (Lahiri 1998). NPIs in other languages, such as English, are also permitted in such contexts (see Ladusaw 1979 and Linebarger 1980). In the discussion below, I will only consider some of the NPIs in Hindi that are permitted in the absence of a negative licensor.

2.2 NPIs in the Context of Questions

The data presented below in 13 and 14 illustrates that some NPIs are permitted in the context of questions. On the other hand, a different set of NPIs is not permitted in the same context. The ungrammatical examples demonstrate this fact. All the questions below are yes/no questions.

(13) a. us   kamre meN   ek   bhii sTuDeNT thaa (kyaa)
        that   room   in   one   even student   was   what
        'Was there even one/any student in that room?'

    b. us   kamre meN   koi   bhii sTuDeNT thaa (kyaa)
        that   room   in   some   even student   was   what
        'Was there even any student in that room?'

    c. aap-ne   kisii bhii sTuDeNT ko   dekh-aa (kyaa)
        you-ERG some   even student   to   see-PERF what
        'Did you see any student?'

    d. aap-ne   kuch   bhii khaa-yaa (kyaa)
        you-ERG something even eat-PERF what
        'Did you eat anything?'

(14) a. ? voh   kabhii   jaa-yegaa (kyaa)
        he   sometime go-FUT   what
        'Will he never go?'

    b. raajiiv abhii   tak   aa-yaa   (kyaa)
        rajiv   now   until come-PERF what
        'Did Rajiv come yet?'

    c. * voh   tum   ko   ek   phuuTi kauRii de-gaa   (kyaa)
        he   you   to   one   broken penny   give-FUT what
        'Will he give you a red cent?'

d. ? vo   Tas   se mas   huaa   (kyaa)
    he   deviate   happen-PERF   what
    'Did he budge an inch?'

e. * raajiiv   tumhaaraa   baal   baaNkaa   kar   sak-egaa   (kyaa)
    rajiv   your   hair   disturb   do   MOD-FUT   what
    'Will Rajiv be able to harm you?'

f. * raajiiv   kii   majaal   ki   vo   kuch   bol-egaa
    rajiv   of   possible that he   something   speak-FUT
    'Is it possible for Rajiv that he could say something?'

The NPIs such as *ek bhii* 'even one/any' in 13a, *koi bhii* 'any' in 13b, *kisii bhii* 'any' in 13c, *kuch bhii* in 13d, and *abhii tak* 'so far' in 14b are permitted in the context of a question interpretation. However, *kabhii* 'never' in 14a, *ek phuuTii kauRii* 'a red cent' in 14c, *Tas se mas na honaa* 'budge an inch' in 14d, *baal na baaNkaa karnaa* 'not being able to make a difference' in 14e, and *majaal na honaa* 'not being within reach' in 14f are not permitted with the same (question) interpretation.

2.3 NPIs in the Context of Conditionals

The data presented below in 15 and 16 illustrates that some NPIs are permitted in the context of conditionals. On the other hand, a different set of NPIs is not permitted in the same context. The ungrammatical examples demonstrate this fact.

(15) a. (agar)   us   kamre   meN   ek   bhii   sTuDeNT   aa-taa   hai   to
         if   that   room   in   one   even   student   come-HAB   is   then

         maiN   aap   ko   bataauNgaa
         I   you   to   tell-FUT

         'I will let you know if even one student comes to that room.'

     b. (agar)   us   kamre   meN   koi   bhii   sTuDeNT   aa-taa   hai
         if   that   room   in   someone   even   student   come-HAB   is

         to   maiN   aap   ko   bataauNgaa
         then   I   you   to   tell-FUT

         'I will let you know if any student comes to that room.'

     c. (agar)   maiN-ne   kisii   bhii   sTuDeNT   ko   dekh-aa   to
         if   I-ERG   someone   even   student   to   see-PERF   then

         usko   piiTuuNgaa
         him   hit-FUT

         'If I see any student, I will beat him up.'

d. (agar) aap-ne   kuch   bhii   khaa-yaa   to   maiN   sab   ko
   if   you-ERG something even   eat-PERF   then I   everybody to

   bataa-uNgaa
   tell-FUT

   'If you eat anything, I will tell everybody.'

e. * agar   voh   kabhii   jaa-yegaa   to   maiN   bataa-uNgaa
     if   he   sometime   go-FUT   then   I   tell-FUT
   'If he never goes, I will let you know.'

(16) a. * (agar) raajiiv abhii tak   aa-yaa   to   maiN   jaa-taa huuN
         if   rajiv   now   until   come-PERF   then I   go-HAB   am
       * 'If Rajiv has come so far then I am going.'

     b. * (agar)   voh   tum   ko   ek   phuuTi   kauRii   de-taa   hai
          if   he   you   to   one   broken   penny   give-HAB is

          to   acchaa   hai
          then   good   is

        * 'If he gives you a red cent, then its okay.'

     c. * (agar) vo   Tas   se   mas   huaa   to   maiN   samajhuuNgaa
          if   he   deviate   happen-PERF   then I   believe-FUT
        * 'If he budges an inch, then I will believe it.'

     d. * (agar) raajiiv   tumhaaraa   baal   baaNkaa   kar   sak-egaa
          if   rajiv   your   hair   disturb   do   MOD-FUT

          to   maiN   samajhuuNgaa
          then   I   believe-FUT

        * 'If Rajiv will be able to harm you, then I will believe it.'

     e. * (agar) raajiiv   kii   majaal   ki   vo   kuch   bol-egaa
          if   rajiv   of   possible   that   he   something   speak-FUT

          to   maiN   samajhuuNgaa
          then   I   believe-FUT

        'If it is possible for Rajiv that he could say something, I will believe it?'

NPIs such as *ek bhii* 'even one/any' in 15a, *koi bhii* 'any' in 15b, *kisii bhii* 'any' in 15c, and *kuch bhii* 'anything' in 15d are permitted in the context of conditional interpretation, whereas *kabhii* 'never' in 15e, *abhii tak* 'so far' in 16a, *ek phuuTii kauRii* 'a red cent' in 16b, *Tas se mas na honaa* 'budge an inch' in 16c, *baal na baaNkaa karnaa* 'not being able to make a difference' in 16d, and *majaal na honaa* 'not being within reach' in 16e are not permitted with the same (conditional) interpretation.

2.4 NPIs in the Context of Modals

The data presented below in 17 and 18 illustrates that some NPIs are permitted in the context of modals. On the other hand, a different set of NPIs is not permitted in the same context. The ungrammatical examples demonstrate this fact.

(17) a. ? us   kamre   meN   ek   bhii sTuDeNT baiTh sak-taa   hai
          that   room   in   one   even student sit   MOD-HAB   is
          'Even one student can sit in that room.'

      b. us   kamre meN   koi   bhii sTuDeNT baiTh   sak-taa   hai
          that   room   in   someone   even student sit   MOD-HAB   is
          'Any student can sit in that room.'

      c. maiN   kisii   bhii sTuDeNT se   mil   sak-taa   huuN
          I   someone   even student with   meet   MOD-HAB   am
          'I can meet with any student.'

      d. aap   kuch   bhii   khaa   sak-te   haiN
          you   anything even   eat   MOD-HAB   are
          'You can eat anything.'

(18) a. * voh   kabhii   jaa   sak-taa   hai
            he   sometimes   go   MOD-HAB   is
            'He can never go.'

      b. * raajiiv   abhii   tak   aa   sak-taa   hai
            rajiv   now   until   come   MOD-HAB   is
          * 'Rajiv can come so far.'

      c. * voh   tum   ko   ek   phuuTi kauRii   de   sak-taa   hai
            he   you   to   one   broken penny   give   MOD-HAB   is
          * 'He can give you a red cent.'

      d. * vo   Tas   se mas   ho   sak-taa   hai
            he   deviate   be   MOD-HAB   is
          * 'He can budge an inch.'

      e. * raajiiv   tumhaaraa   baal   baaNkaa   kar   sak-taa   hai
            rajiv   your   hair   disturb   do   MOD-HAB   is
          * 'Rajiv can be able to harm you.'

      f. * raajiiv   kii   majaal   ki   vo   kuch   bol   sak-taa   hai
            rajiv   of   possible that he   something   speak   can-HAB   is
          'It is possible for Rajiv that he can say something.'

Just as in the distribution of NPIs in the two contexts discussed above, the data given above illustrates that some NPIs can appear in the context of modals even in the absence of an overt negation marker, while a different set of NPIs is not permitted in the same context. NPIs such as *ek bhii* 'even one/any' in 17a, *koi bhii* 'any' in 17b, *kisii bhii* 'any' in 17c, and *kuch bhii* 'anything' in 17d are permitted in the context of a modal. However, *kabhii* 'never' in 18a, *abhii tak* 'so far' in 18b, *ek phuuTii kauRii* 'a red cent' in 18c, *Tas se mas na honaa* 'budge an inch' in 18d, *baal na baaNkaa karnaa* 'not being able to make a difference' in 18e, and *majaal na honaa* 'not being within reach' in 18f are not permitted with the same (modal) interpretation. We also observe that *ek bhii* 'even one/any' in 17a is slightly marginal. This leads to a separate implication that I will discuss shortly.

2.5 NPIs in the Context of Adversative Predicates

The data presented below in 19 and 20 illustrates that some NPIs are permitted in the context of adversative predicates. On the other hand, a different set of NPIs is not permitted in the same context. The ungrammatical examples demonstrate this fact.

(19) a. | ? mujhe | aaScarya | hai | ki | kal | ek | bhii sTuDeNT |
|---|---|---|---|---|---|---|
| I-DAT | surprise | is | that | yesterday | one | even student |

  aa-yaa
  come-PERF

  'I am surprised that even one/any student came yesterday.'

b. | mujhe | aaScarya | hai | ki | kal | koi | bhii sTuDeNT |
|---|---|---|---|---|---|---|
| I-DAT | surprise | is | that | yesterday | some | even student |

  aa-yaa
  come-PERF

  'I am surprised that any student came yesterday.'

c. | mujhe | aaScarya | hai | ki | kal | maiN-ne | kisii | bhii |
|---|---|---|---|---|---|---|---|
| I-DAT | surprise | is | that | yesterday | I-ERG | some | even |

  sTuDeNT   ko   dekh-aa
  student   to   see-PERF
  'I am surprised that I saw any student yesterday.'

d. mujhe aaScarya hai ki kal aap-ne kuch bhii
 I-DAT   is that yesterday you-ERG something even

khaa-yaa
eat-PERF

'I am surprised that you ate anything.'

(20) a. * mujhe aaScarya hai ki voh kabhii gayaa
     I-DAT surprise is that he sometime go-PERF
     'I am surprised that he never went.'

   b. * mujhe aaScarya hai ki raajiiv abhii tak aa-yaa
     I-DAT surprise is that rajiv now until come-PERF
     'I am surprised that Rajiv came so far.'

   c. * mujhe aaScarya hai ki us-ne tum ko ek phuuTi kauRii
     I-DAT surprise is that he-ERG you to one broken penny

d-ii
give-PERF

    * 'I am surprised that he gave a red cent.'

   d. * mujhe aaScarya hai hai vo Tas se mas huaa
     I-DAT surprise is that that deviate   happen-PERF
     * 'I am surprised that he was ready to budge an inch.'

   e. * mujhe aaScarya hai ki raajiiv tumhaaraa baal baaNkaa
     I-DAT surprise is that rajiv your   hair disturb

kar sak-aa
do MOD-PERF

'I am surprised that Rajiv will be able to harm you.'

   f. * mujhe aaScarya hai ki raajiiv kii majaal ki
     I-DAT surprise is that rajiv of possible that

vo kuch   bol-egaa
he something something

'I am surprised that it is possible for Rajiv that he could say something.'

The NPIs such as *ek bhii* 'even one/any' in 19a, *koi bhii* 'any' in 19b, *kisii bhii* 'any' in 19c, and *kuch bhii* 'anything' in 19d are permitted in the context of an adversative predicate, whereas *kabhii* 'never' in 20a, *abhii tak* 'so far' in 20b, *ek phooTii kauRii* 'a red cent' in 20c, *Tas se mas na honaa* 'budge an inch' in 20d, *baal na baaNkaa karnaa* 'not being able to make a difference' in 20e, and *majaal na honaa* 'not being within reach' in 20f are not permitted with the same (adversative) interpretation.

In the discussion so far on the distribution of NPIs, we observe a crucial and systematic distinction between NPIs. We can say that there are two distinct groups of NPIs and can categorize these two patterns as follows: all the NPIs discussed so far are permitted in the presence of a clause mate negation marker, but only *koi bhii* 'any,' *kisii bhii* 'any,' and *kuch bhii* 'anything' are permitted in the context of questions, conditionals, modals, or adversative predicates. NPIs of the other class, namely *ek bhii* 'even one/any,' *kabhii* 'never,' *abhii tak* 'so far,' *ek phuuTii kauRii* 'a red cent,' *Tas se mas na honaa* 'budge an inch,' *baal na baaNkaa karnaa* 'not being able to make a difference,' and *majaal na honaa* 'not being within reach' are not permitted without a clause mate negation. In the next chapter I will discuss more differences between these NPIs and show that the two distinct groups are syntactically different. In the following section, I discuss some of the previously proposed analyses of NPI licensing.

3. NPI LICENSING

This section deals with the licensing facts regarding NPIs, namely the presence of a negative licensor and its structural position in the clause structure. In order for an NPI to be what is technically known as "licensed" in all languages, there must be a negative licensor in the sentence, except in the contexts discussed above. In this section, I present some of the previous analyses of NPI licensing and discuss two major accounts of such licensing, namely LF movement of negation markers and reconstruction of NPIs to the original position, addressing some potential problems with these accounts.

3.1 Some Previous Accounts of NPI Licensing

There have been several proposals stating conditions on the licensing of NPIs: e.g. Jackendoff (1969), Lasnik (1975), Ladusaw (1979), Linebarger (1980 and 1987), Mahajan (1990a), Progovac (1994), Haegeman (1995), and Lahiri (1998). I will discuss Jackendoff (1969) and Lasnik (1975), Linebarger (1980), Ladusaw (1979), Progovac (1994), and Laka (1994) in detail below.

3.1.1 Jackendoff (1969) and Lasnik (1975):

The following examples of NPI licensing show an interaction between NPIs and surface structure:

(21) a.   * Anybody does not play cricket.
    b.   * The man who did not come watched any movie.
    c.   I did not ask anybody to play cricket.
    d.   [I did not think [that anybody would play cricket]].

The ungrammaticality of the examples in 21a and 21b clearly shows that the negative licensor must precede and command the NPI. The example in 21d shows that the negative licensor may sometimes be in the higher clause and still license the NPI.

Jackendoff (1969) and Lasnik (1975) argue for a surface structure condition in the licensing of NPIs on the basis of the data in 21. They state their conditions on the licensing of NPIs differently. Jackendoff suggests that the negation marker originates in its surface structure position and moves up in the tree by an interpretive rule, thus taking wider scope. Later he modifies the rule and invokes precede and command relation. That is to say that everything preceded and commanded by a negative marker or a negative incorporated quantifier is in the scope of that negative marker. In Lasnik, on the other hand, a "Not Scope Rule" takes care of the analysis of the scope of negation. This rule provides a [+Neg] feature to quantifiers, quantificational adverbs, etc. Lasnik's account predicts that NPIs, which are inherently referential, will be acceptable if they occur to the right of and are commanded by a negation marker in surface structure. In addition to being present, the negative licensor must be higher than the NPI in the clause structure. Thus, according to both analyses (Jackendoff 1969 and Lasnik 1975), a condition on the acceptability of NPIs is that they occur in the scope of negation markers. The scope of a negation marker maximally includes everything to the right of and commanded by a lexical negation marker in surface structure.

Linebarger (1980) shows the potential problems with both Jackendoff (1969) and Lasnik (1975). One of her objections to the surface structure account of NPI licensing concerns NPIs that are permitted in the absence of an overt negative marker in the contexts of questions, modality, conditionals, and adversative predicates, to name a few. She cites various examples to demonstrate that the surface structure accounts of Jackendoff and Lasnik are not sufficient to account for the licensing conditions on NPIs. For example, she claims that the acceptability of an NPI in an embedded sentence with a negation marker in the higher clause, as in 22, depends upon meaning and not just upon the syntactic configuration of the sentence.

(22) a. I didn't say that I had ever been to Istanbul.
  b. * I did not add/yell that I had ever been to Istanbul.
  c. I do not think that she can help doing what she does.
  d. * I do not regret that she can help doing what she does.

According to Linebarger, all the examples in 22 contain a negation marker in the higher clause. Hence, if the scope of negation includes everything that is preceded and commanded by the negation marker, the examples in 22 should all be acceptable. The fact that 22b and 22d are not acceptable shows that the scope of negation does not include everything to the right of and commanded by negation.

I would add here that the surface structure accounts of NPI licensing of Jackendoff and Lasnik are not sufficient to account for the Hindi data like the example in 23. It is a well-known fact of Hindi and many other languages that NPIs are permitted in subject position.

(23) ek   bhii   laRkii   nahiiN   aa-yii
    one   even   girl   NEG   come-PERF
    'Any girl did not come.' (None of the girls/not even one girl came.)

In 23 the negative licensor *nahiiN* does not precede the NPI *ek bhii* 'even one.' However, the NPI is still licensed.

3.1.2 Linebarger (1980):

Linebarger clearly assumes that the licensing conditions on NPIs cannot be stated only in syntactic terms. She argues that the distribution of NPIs in English reflects an overlap of syntax and pragmatics. Her analysis of NPI licensing heavily relies on Baker (1970), who proposes that in the presence of an overt negation marker, NPIs are licensed under the notion of c-command, while in the absence of an overt negation marker, NPIs are licensed by implicature (pragmatic constraints).

Linebarger's analysis has two parts. The first part deals with the cases of licensing in the presence of an overt negation marker, and the second part deals with the cases of licensing of NPIs in the absence of an overt negation marker. In the first part, she formulates a syntactic constraint, the "Immediate Scope Constraint" (ISC), which applies at LF. The ISC can be simply stated as follows: NPIs are acceptable in a sentence if at LF an NPI is in the immediate scope of negation. The NPI must occur in a proposition that is in the entire scope of negation, and within this proposition there must be no "logical elements" intervening between the NPI and negation, where "logical elements" are defined as elements capable of entering into scope ambiguities. The ISC accounts for the following example:

(24) He did not eat anything.

Let us consider the following example to see further the application of the ISC:

(25) a. * He did not budge an inch because she was pushed (but because he fell).
      b. NOT CAUSE (S-1, S-2)
         It is not true that S-1 causes S-2.

      c. * John did not give a red cent to every charity.
      d. NOT ∀x (charity, x) (John gave a red cent to x)

      e. John did not move because anyone pushed him.
      f. IMPLICATURE: No one pushed him.

      g. I was surprised that she contributed a red cent.
      h. IMPLICATURE: I had expected her not to contribute a red cent.

According to Linebarger's ISC, the examples in 25a and 25c are not acceptable, as logical elements intervene between the negation marker and the NPI at LF, so that the NPIs are not in the immediate scope of the negation marker. In 25b, the predicate CAUSE intervenes between the negative marker NOT and S-2, which makes the NPI *budge an inch* impossible in S-2. The same applies at LF in 25c, where the universal quantifier *every* is present in the immediate scope of the negation marker. In other words, the presence of a universal quantifier in the immediate scope of a negation marker at LF blocks the licensing of an NPI.

The second part of Linebarger's analysis, pragmatic implicature, is meant to account for the cases that cannot be accounted for by the first part, such as the examples in 25e and 25g. In short, Linebarger's approach makes the negative polarity licensing phenomenon a context sensitive operation beyond syntax. However, a close look at her proposal suggests that all negative polarity items require a negative licensor, either an overt negation marker or a context dependent negative implicature.

Linebarger's proposal involves two abstract assumptions: (a) some sort of LF operation and (b) some sort of abstract calculation of negative implicature.

This proposal may have an advantage over the surface structure accounts of NPI licensing of Jackendoff (1969) and Lasnik (1975) for a language like English. However, it may not carry over to languages such as Hindi, and it is nevertheless problematic for English as well. If the licensing of NPIs and the scope of negation are determined at LF, it is not clear what prohibits the occurrence of NPIs in subject position in English.

3.1.3. Ladusaw (1979):

Ladusaw proposes as a requirement for the licensing of NPIs that the NPIs be within the logical scope of a licensing element, where a licensing element is a subclass of the downward entailing expressions. This predicts examples such as 26 to be grammatical. To eliminate such undesirable possibilities, Ladusaw puts forth another constraint: that the licensor must precede the clause mate licensee. In other words, a licensor must c-command the licensee at surface structure.

(26) a.   * He read any of the stories to none of the children.
     b.   * Any of the teachers did not attend the meeting.

Ladusaw's is an attempt to reduce the licensing of NPIs to a purely semantic phenomenon, namely downward entailment, and it assumes that negation is a member of the subclass of downward entailing expressions. In this system, an expression is downward entailing if it licenses inferences in its scope from superset to subset. Consider the following examples in 27:

(27) a.   Mary did not eat fruits. [NOT A]
     b.   Mary did not eat apples. [NOT B]

This is an instance of downward entailment. Under the assumptions of downward entailment, Ladusaw proposes the following constraint: an NPI must be in the scope of a downward entailing element (such as negation), and if the downward entailing element is in the same clause as the NPI, it must precede the NPI. This constraint predicts the following acceptability judgments:

(28) a.   Mary did not eat anything.
     b.   * Mary ate anything.

(29) a.   If you have any pet you will be allowed in.
     b.   Everyone who has any pets will be allowed in.

This analysis accounts for the presence of conditional and universal quantifiers co-occurring with NPIs, as in example 29 and for other contexts where NPIs are permitted.

Ladusaw's analysis assumes that downward entailment will work in all languages in the same way that it does in English and that NPIs will be licensed in every language in the same way that they are licensed in English. The first part of the assumption may be true, although it needs to be verified cross-linguistically; however, the licensing of NPIs definitely does not work in Hindi the way it works in English. For example, NPIs in subject positions are licensed in Hindi, as in 30, and the assumptions of this analysis does not account for such instances.

(30) ek   bhii   laRkii   nahiiN   aa-yii
     one   even   girl   NEG   come-PERF
     'Any girl did not come.' (None of the girls/not even one girl came.)

3.1.4 Progovac (1994)

Progovac's analysis of NPI licensing involves a transfer of the assumptions of Binding Theory to polarity licensing. She claims that a binding theoretic analysis of NPI licensing accounts for all the environments of NPI licensing in 31, where English NPIs do not seem to adhere to any locality requirement.

(31) a. John did not meet *anyone.*
     b. Mary did not say that John had met *anyone.*
     c. Did John meet *anyone?*
     d. If John met *anyone,* he will inform us.
     e. I doubt that John met *anyone.*
     f. John does not think that Mary said that she had met *anyone.*

Progovac suggests that NPIs are licensed under the assumptions of Binding Principles A and B of the Binding Theory. NPI licensing obeys the following universal and parameter:

> "All NPIs must be bound and are subject to Binding Principles. Some NPIs are subject to Principle-A (English, Italian and Chinese NPIs) and some are subject to Principle-B (Serbian NPIs). Some NPIs raise at LF whereas others do not." (Progovac 1994)

Licensing of NPIs obeys some kind of locality restriction. The antecedent for an anaphor in English is an NP in the Spec position of IP, whereas the antecedent for an NPI in English is a functional category (negation) as the head of its own projection negation in INFL or as a negative operator in COMP. Let us consider the following examples:

(32) a. John did not meet *anyone*.
    b. Did John meet *anyone?*
    c. If John met *anyone,* he will inform us.
    d. I doubt that John met *anyone*.

In 32a, the negation marker *not* binds the NPI *anyone* under the assumptions of Principle-A of the Binding Theory. The NPI *anyone* is in the governing category of the negation marker *not*. The negation marker *not* is in the head of NegP or in I, and subsequently it c-commands the NPI *anyone*. In the rest of the examples in 32, it is argued that there is an empty negative licensor or operator present in COMP that binds the NPI *anyone* in the context of the question in 32b, the conditional in 32c, and the adversative predicate in 32d.

    Progovac allows NPIs to move at LF in order to be in the governing category of the negative licensor in the case of the long-distance licensing of NPIs. Let us consider the following examples:

(33) a. Mary did not say that John had met *anyone*.
       LF Representation:
    b. Mary did not say [$_{CP}$ anyone$_i$ [$_{C'}$ that [$_{IP}$ John had met t$_{i}$.]]]

    c. John does not think that Mary said that she had met *anyone*.
       LF Representation:
    d. John does not think [$_{CP}$ anyone$_i$ [$_{C'}$ that [$_{IP}$ Mary said [$_{CP}$ t$_i$ [$_{C'}$ that [$_{IP}$ she had met t$_{i}$.]]]]]]

In 33, the NPI *anyone* is allowed to move higher at LF to be in the governing category of the negation marker *not*. The examples in 33b and 33d give the LF representations of 33a and 33c, respectively.

    Progovac's analysis is designed to account for the two types of NPIs in Serbo-Croatian. Progovac calls them NI-NPIs and I-NPIs. These names are based on their prefixes. The NI-NPIs begin with the *ni*–prefix, whereas the I-NPIs begin with the *i*–prefix. Morphologically they are complex units. They are formed from the combination of a negative prefix *n*–and wh–phrases, as shown in 34 below.

(34) NI-NPIs   I-NPIs
    ni-ko   (no one)   i-ko   (anyone)
    ni-Sta   (nothing)   i-Sta   (anything)
    ni-kud   (nowhere)   i-kud   (anywhere)

NI-NPIs occur only in the presence of an overt clause mate negative licensor. If the negation marker is not within the same clause as the NPI, the sentence results in ungrammaticality. In other words, NI-NPIs cannot be licensed long-distance. Consider the following examples from Progovac:

(35) a. milan   ne   vidi   nista
       Milan   NEG   sees   nothing
       'Milan cannot see anything.'

    b. * milan   vidi   nista
        Milan   sees   nothing

    c. * milan   ne   tvrdi [da   marija   poznaje   nikio-ga]
        Milan   NEG   sees   that Mary   knows   none
        'Milan does not claim that Mary knows no one.'

In 35a, the NPI and the negative licensor are in the same clause; hence, the sentence is grammatical. In 35b, no negative licensor is in the sentence, whereas in 35c, the negative licensor is in the higher clause. In both cases, the sentences are ungrammatical, which shows that the NPIs and the negative licensors are required to be in the same clause for the sentence to be grammatical.

With various examples, Progovac also shows that the clause mate negative licensor can license more than one NI-NPI and also that it can license not only object NPIs, but also other arguments (including pre-verbal subjects) and adjunct NPIs.

Though I-NPIs also require a negative licensor for their legitimate occurrence in a sentence, the negative licensor and the NPI are not permitted to be in the same clause. If they are in the same clause, then the sentence is ungrammatical. In other words, I-NPIs can only be licensed long-distance by a negative licensor in a higher clause. Consider the following examples from Progovac:

(36) a. * milan   ne   zna   ista
        Milan   NEG   knows anything
        'Milan does not know anything.'

    b. milan   ne   tvrdi [da   marija   poznaje   iko-ga]
       Milan   NEG   sees   that Mary   knows   none
       'Milan does not claim that Mary knows no one.'

The sentence in 36a is ungrammatical, as the negative licensor and the I-NPI are both in the same clause. On the other hand, the example in 36b is grammatical, as the negative licensor is in the higher clause and the I-NPI is in the lower clause. Thus, the example in 36 shows that the I-NPI and the negative licensor cannot be clause mates.

Progovac's approach to the licensing of NPIs is summarized below. Along the lines of "Generalized Binding" (Aoun 1985 and 1986), Progovac argues that NPIs in Serbo-Croatian are anaphoric. To capture the distributional properties of Serbo-Croatian NI-NPIs and I-NPIs, Progovac suggests that NI-NPIs are subject to Principle-A and that the I-NPIs are subject to both Principle-A and Principle-B. I-NPIs obey restrictions on Principle-B at surface structure and obey the requirements of Principle A at LF. The negative licensor is not a clause mate of I-NPIs at surface structure; thus, I-NPIs move at LF to be bound within the governing category.

Progovac assumes that NI-NPIs do not move at LF. They are A-bar anaphors and are in the governing category, which contains the NPI, its governor, and the accessible subject (agreement in INFL). In the absence of a clause mate negative licensor, NI-NPIs are not bound, as the binding requirements are not met. When the negative licensor is in the higher clause, the NI-NPI is not bound either. Again, in such cases, the binding requirements are not met, for NI-NPIs do not move at LF.

I-NPIs are A-bar pronominals. The pronominal requirement is satisfied at s-structure, but the I-NPIs are not bound, as the negative licensor cannot be a clause mate of I-NPIs. Thus, they move at LF to satisfy anaphoric requirements and become clause mates with the negative licensor, as they are both in the same governing category at LF.

Progovac shows with various examples that the displacement of the NPIs at LF, to enable them to be in the governing category of the negation marker, does not violate any condition on displacement.

Progovac discusses Serbo-Croatian NPIs in non-negative contexts and shows that only I-NPIs are allowed in non-negative contexts such as questions, conditionals, and adversative predicates.

In the context of questions:

(37) a. da   li   iko   dolazi
        that que   anyone   comes
        'Did anyone come?'

     b. * da   li   niko   dolazi
          that que   anyone   comes
          'Did anyone come?'
          (From Progovac 1988:114, as in Uribe-Echevarria 1994)

In the context of conditionals:

(38) a. ako   milan   voli   iko-ga   bi-ce   sreean   u   zivot
         if   Milan   loves   anyone-acc   be-FUT   happy   in   life-LOC
         'If Milan loves anyone, he will be happy.'

   b. * ako   milan   voli   niko-ga   bi-ce   sreean   u   zivot
          if   Milan   loves   anyone-acc   be-FUT   happy   in   life-LOC
          'If Milan loves anyone, he will be happy.'
          (From Progovac 1988:114R, as in Uribe-Echevarria 1994)

In the context of adversative predicates:

(39) a. sumanja-m   da   je   ikada   bio   u   kin-i
         doubt-ISG   that   is   ever   been   in   China
         'I doubt that he has ever been to China.'

   b. * sumanja-m   da   je   nikada   bio   u   kin-i
          doubt-ISG   that   is   ever   been   in   China
          'I doubt that he has ever been to China.'
          (From Progovac 1988:114, as in Uribe-Echevarria 1994)

The examples in 37, 38, and 39 show that NI-NPIs are not allowed in the context of questions, as in 37b, conditionals, as in 38b, or adversative predicates, as in 39b. However, I-NPIs are allowed in the same contexts. NI-NPIs are more like Hindi strong NPIs in terms of locality constraints and their occurrence in the contexts stated above. Chapter Five explores further the implications of the occurrence of NPIs in such contexts in Hindi.

To account for the occurrence of NPIs in non-negative contexts, Progovac proposes that there is a polarity operator in the spec of CP in all such contexts, as shown in 40.

(40) a. $[_{CP}$ op $[_{C'}$ $[_{IP}$ ... I-NPI ...]
     b. $[_{CP}$ op $[_{C'}$ $[_{IP}$ I-NPI$_i$ $[_{IP}$ ... t$_i$ ...]

The governing category in these cases is the first maximal projection that contains INFL and the NPIs. I-NPIs are still not bound at LF. However, they can move at LF and be bound in the above-stated governing category. In this case, the I-NPI is adjoined to IP (as shown in 40b), to be posited in the same governing category as its licensor in questions, conditionals, and adversative predicates.

There are several objections to this binding theoretic analysis of NPI licensing. First of all, just like Jackendoff (1969), Lasnik (1975), Ladusaw

(1979), and Linebarger (1980), Progovac (1994) does not account for cross-linguistic variation. For example, Hindi allows NPIs to be licensed in subject position, where the negative licensor does not c-command the NPI. In addition, Progovac's analysis of the displacement of NPIs is not motivated by any other reason than the requirement for putting the NPIs in the governing category of their negative licensors.

3.1.5 Laka (1994)

So far, we have seen many examples where the negative licensor occurs in the higher clause and the NPI occurs in the lower clause. To account for such cases, Laka provides an analysis that assumes the presence of a negative COMP. She differs from Progovac in that Progovac assumes an operator in CP as licensor, whereas Laka assumes a negative complementizer.

There are two reasons for Laka to propose such a hypothesis (Uribe-Echevarria 1994). First, it accounts for the occurrence of NPIs in sentential subjects, as in 41a, where the NPI within the sentential subject is not c-commanded by the negative licensor, and of NPIs in sentential objects, as in 41c. Second, it accounts for the asymmetry in the licensing of NPIs by a negative licensor and in the contexts of adversative predicates, as in 41e.

(41) a. That anyone might do anything like this never occurred to John.

   b. $[_{CP}$ [Neg] COMP $[\ldots $ I-NPI $\ldots]]_i$ Neg V t_i

   c. John did not say that he saw anything.

   d. $\ldots$ aux Neg V $[_{CP}$ [Neg] COMP $[_{IP} \ldots $ I-NPI $\ldots]]$

   e. John denied that Mary ate anything.

   f. $\ldots$ V $[_{CP}$ [Neg] COMP $[_{IP} \ldots $ I-NPI $\ldots]]$

Evidence in support of the presence of a negated COMP comes from the overt difference displayed by clausal complements in Basque. Sentential complements in negative clauses in Basque can appear either with the–*e(la)* or—*(e)nik* suffix. A sentential complement in a negative clause with the–*e(la)* suffix is interpreted as out of the scope of the negative marker, whereas a sentential complement in a negative clause with the–*(e)nik* suffix is interpreted as within the scope of negation. As the above-stated distinction predicts, NPIs are allowed only in sentential complements with the–*(e)nik* suffix. Consider the examples in 42:

(42) a. ez   dut   uste   [inor   etorri   denik]
          NEG   aux   think   anybody   come   aux-enik
          'I do not think that anybody came.'

    b. * ez   dut   uste   [inor   etorri   dela]
          NEG   aux   think   anybody   come   aux-enik
          'I do not think that anybody came.'
          (From Uribe-Echevarria 1994:174)

As the contrast between 42a and 42b shows, the NPI is permitted when the sentential complement contains the–*(e)nik* suffix. Since NPIs are licensed only with–*(e)nik* complements, Laka argues, this provides evidence for the presence of a negative COMP for the licensing of NPIs.

Like the analyses of Jackendoff (1969), Lasnik (1975), Ladusaw (1979), Linebarger (1980), and Progovac (1994), the above analysis does not account for the fact that NPIs are licensed in subject positions in Hindi, where, under the assumptions of these analyses, the negative licensor does not appear to c-command the NPI, as in 43.

(43) koi   bhii   nahiiN   aa-yaa
       someone   even   NEG   come-PERF
       'No one came.'

An assumption of negative COMP does not work for Hindi. I entertain this idea in Chapter Five with reference to the licensing of NPIs in the absence of an overt negation marker and show that it does not work.

3.1.6 Mahajan (1990a):

Having discussed the analyses mentioned above and the potential problems with them in dealing with languages such as Hindi, I will discuss Mahajan's account for the licensing of NPIs in Hindi. He argues for an obligatory displacement of negation in Hindi at LF. In order to account for the data in 43, Mahajan's account offers upward LF movement of the negative licensor, so that it is in a c-commanding relation with the NPI.

Let us first look at the mechanism adopted in Mahajan for the upward LF movement of negative licensors. Mahajan argues that the negative licensor moves higher at LF, adjoins to the finite IP, and thereby licenses the NPI, as it does not c-command the NPI at s-structure. Let us consider the following sentences from Mahajan:

(44) a. koi bhii t$_i$ nahiiN khaa-taa thaa sabzii$_i$

   someone even NEG eat-HAB was vegetable

   'No one used to eat vegetables.'

  b. * koi bhii t$_i$ nahiiN khaa-taa sabzii$_i$ thaa

    someone even NEG eat-HAB vegetable was

    'No one used to eat vegetables.'

  c.

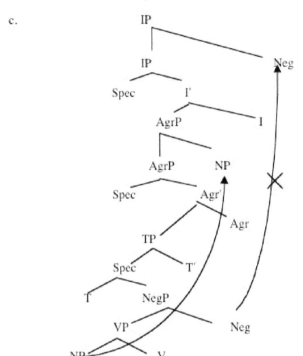

   The example in 44a is grammatical, whereas the one in 44b is ungrammatical. The ungrammatical example is structurally illustrated with the help of the tree in 44c. Through these examples, Mahajan shows that the movement of a negative licensor at LF is obligatory. Once the movement takes place, the negative licensor is in a position from which it can c-command the NPI. In 44a and 44b, he provides evidence for such movement. Due to the presence of the right-scrambled NP *sabzii* 'vegetable,' which is adjoined to AgrP, the movement of Neg is blocked further. The presence of the right-adjoined scrambled phrase that is lower than the finite I, in 44b, introduces a barrier that blocks the movement of the negative licensor at LF to a position where it can be governed by finite I (Laka 1989). Hence, 44b is ungrammatical. The ungrammaticality of 44b is due to the fact that the negation marker is not in a position to move to be adjoined to IP. This shows that the movement of Neg is obligatory. On the other hand, if the right-scrambled DO is adjoined to the finite I (i.e. higher than the AgrP, as in 44a), then there is no barrier to block the Neg raising. Thus, in such cases, the Neg can c-command the NPI.

Later in this section, I will present a critique of this analysis. I will discuss an alternative way of dealing with Hindi NPIs. Such an alternative involves syntactic operations such as reconstruction (Barss 1986 and Chomsky 1995, among others). In the reconstruction approach, the NPI could be assumed to move lower. Let us consider first the facts about NPIs in Hindi.

3.2 Facts about NPI Licensing in Hindi

NPIs in Hindi—elements such as *koi bhii* 'any,' as in 45a, *kisii bhii* 'any,' as in 45b, *kabhii nahiiN* 'never,' as in 45c, *ek bhii* 'even one,' as in 45d, etc.— require a negative licensor for their legitimate presence in a sentence, as shown in 45.

(45) a. koi   bhii   nahiiN   aa-yaa
         someone   even   NEG   come-PERF
         'No one came.'

     b. maiN-ne   kisii   bhii   sTuDeNT   ko   nahiiN   dekh-aa
         I-ERG   some   even   student   to   NEG   see-PERF
         'I did not see any student.'

     c. maiN   kabhii   dillii   nahiiN   gayaa
         I   sometime   delhi   NEG   go-PERF
         'I never went to Delhi.'

     d. maiN-ne   ek   bhii   kahaanii   nahiiN   paRh-ii
         I-ERG   one   even   story   NEG   read-PERF
         'I did not read any story.'

Most studies on the licensing of negative polarity items (Bhatia 1978, Lasnik 1981, Laka 1989, Mahajan 1990a, and Benmamoun 1997 and 2000) agree that NPIs are licensed under certain well-defined conditions. Such conditions, in one form or another, all include that the negative licensor must c-command the NPI.

In Hindi, the NPI occurs higher than the negative licensor in the structural assumptions of most of the analyses of the NPIs (e.g. Mahajan 1990a). The following structure, in 45e, illustrates:

(45) e.

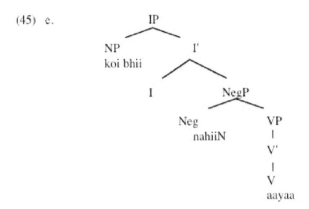

The structure in 45e shows that the subject position is higher than negation in the clause structure. The subject occurs in the Spec of IP, whereas negation occurs as the head of the NegP (as most of the studies assume). Thus, negation does not seem to c-command the NPI.

To account for this problem, there are two possible alternative accounts. Both assume some sort of displacement of the negative licensor at LF, so that it is in a position to license an NPI in a language such as Hindi. In the first approach, the negative licensor has been argued to move at LF (Mahajan 1990a), whereas in the second approach, the NPI is argued to move lower under the assumptions of reconstruction (Barss 1986 and Chomsky 1995, among others). Later in this chapter, I present a critique of these approaches to NPI licensing that involve covert displacement. The critique shows how both the approaches run into problems in providing an explanatory account for the licensing of NPIs in Hindi.

3.3 LF Movement of Negation in Hindi for NPI Licensing

It has been assumed in most of the studies of NPI licensing that negation occurs in the functional domain of the clause structure at a position lower than the Spec of IP. The occurrence in some cases of the negative licensor lower than the NPI (in particular when the NPI occurs in subject position) poses problems for an analysis of NPI licensing that requires a negative licensor to c-command the NPI or to be higher than the NPI in clause structure. In order to account for the data in 45, there are two available analyses, discussed briefly above. Both these analyses require covert displacement. The first account (Mahajan 1990a) offers upward LF movement of a negative licensor, so it can be in a c-commanding relation with the NPI, whereas the second possible approach, which assumes reconstruction (Barss 1986,

Chomsky 1995, etc.), argues for the reconstruction of the clause containing the NPI to its original position.

As we have seen earlier, the occurrence of NPIs in subject position in Hindi poses a problem for all the proposals discussed so far (Jackendoff 1969, Lasnik 1975, Ladusaw 1979, Linebarger 1980, Laka 1994, and Progovac 1994). However, most of these analyses do assume some sort of c-command, in the form of command (Lasnik 1975), the assumption that NPIs are to the right of negative licensors (Jackendoff 1969), the Immediate Scope Constraint (Linebarger 1980), or the requirement that the NPI and the negative licensor be in the same governing category (Progovac 1994). Yet none of these conditions on the licensing of NPIs provides any account for the presence of NPIs in the subject position in Hindi. To provide a c-commanding licensor for NPIs in subject position, Mahajan (1990a) invokes an obligatory movement of negation markers at LF. This puts the negation marker in a position from which it can c-command NPIs in any position (subject or object).

3.4 Problems with the LF Movement–Based Account of NPI Licensing

The analysis in Mahajan (1990a) faces several problems. Mahajan, following Lasnik and Saito (1992), claims that Neg does not raise at LF to adjoin to IP, due to the barrier created by the adjunction of the right-scrambled DO to the AgrP. Recall Mahajan's (1990a) analysis, as discussed above. I repeat the crucial data set from his analysis below.

(46) a. koi   bhii t$_i$ nahiiN   khaa-taa   thaa   sabzi$_i$
        someone   even   NEG   eat-HAB   was   vegetable
        'No one used to eat vegetables.'

     b. * koi   bhii   t$_i$ nahiiN   khaa-taa   sabzi$_i$ thaa
        someone   even   NEG   eat-HAB   vegetable   was
        'No one used to eat vegetables.'

The example in 46b is ungrammatical because the barrier blocks Neg raising at LF. For Mahajan, the ungrammaticality of 46b is evidence for the obligatory movement of Neg at LF: Neg must move at LF in order to license the NPI.

Mahajan (1994) provides evidence in favor of the claim that adjunction to a maximal projection creates an A-bar node and involves a non-L-related position. He shows that scrambling operations in Hindi involve both Argument Shift (movement to an a/L related position) and Adjunction (movement to a non-a/L related position). The scrambling in 46b is an instance of adjunction to AgrP. Since adjunction creates an A-bar node, this particular instance of scrambling is A-bar scrambling. Elements moved to an A-bar position can reconstruct (they can be interpreted in their original position) at LF. Thus, the adjunction of the right-scrambled DO in 46b can reconstruct, so it does not seem to be a potential barrier for the LF raising of Neg. The movement of Neg at LF does not seem, therefore, to be an obligatory condition. If the movement of Neg is not obligatory and we claim that it still moves, such movement becomes a mere stipulation in order to provide a c-commanding licensor for the licensing of NPIs. Furthermore, 46b appears to be ungrammatical for reasons independent of the requirement on NPI licensing, as shown in 47a, and independent of negation, as seen in 47b. At this point I do not provide any analysis for why 47a and 47b are ungrammatical.

(47) a.
?/* raam t$_i$ nahiiN   khaa-taa   sabzi$_i$ thaa
ram   NEG   eat-HAB   vegetable   was
'Ram did not used to eat vegetables.'

b.
?/* raam t$_i$ khaa-taa   sabzi$_i$ thaa
ram   eat-HAB   vegetable   was
'Ram did not used to eat vegetables.'

So far we have seen that this analysis is inadequate in that it fails to provide an account for the empirical data. Conceptually, it is not clear what motivates the movement of the negative licenser other than the need to be in a position where the c-command requirement is maintained.

There are further problems with the analysis that requires the raising of negation at LF. The movement of the negative licensor is an instance of head movement, which is considered to be local, whereas an NPI in Hindi can scramble long-distance, as in 41. If the movement of Neg is an obligatory condition for the licensing of NPIs, this analysis predicts that heads may move long-distance; otherwise it has no account for sentences such as the one in 48. Note that the long-distance movement of heads violates the Head-Movement Constraint (HMC).

(48) [kisii   ko   bhii]$_i$ sariitaa-ne   kahaa   ki   raajiiv-ne t$_i$
someone   to   even   sarita-ERG   say-PERF   that rajiv-ERG

yahaaN   nahiiN   dekh-aa
here   NEG   see-PERF

'Sarita said that Rajiv did not see anyone here.'

Thus, Mahajan's (1990a) analysis predicts that there is no limit on the position to which heads can move. The grammaticality of 48 does not involve any violation of HMC, as the scrambled NPI *kisii ko bhii* 'anyone' is licensed prior to scrambling. I discuss this in detail in section 4 of this chapter.

3.5 Reconstruction of Clause for NPI Licensing

There is an alternative way to look at the licensing of NPIs in Hindi. This alternative, following the assumptions of reconstruction (Barss 1986 and Chomsky 1995, among others), posits LF reconstruction of the scrambled NPI to a position where it can be c-commanded. Reconstruction, in the theory of grammar, according to Barss (2001), is a phenomenon exhibiting complex interactions among representations of movement operations and principles determining the possibility or impossibility of referential relations among NPs. In other words, reconstruction is the syntactic operation by which a movement is undone (reconstructed), so that the structure returns to its pre-movement representation (as if the movement had not taken place). Let us consider the following examples from Hindi, to demonstrate the process of reconstruction:

(49) a. sariitaa-ne apne aap ko kabhii   khuubsuurat nahiiN samjh-aa
          sarita-ERG self   to sometime pretty   NEG   consider-PERF
          'Sarita never considered herself pretty.'

     b. apne aap ko$_i$ sariitaa-ne t$_i$ kabhii   khuubsuurat nahiiN samjh-aa
          self   to sarita-ERG   sometime pretty   NEG   consider-PERF
          'Sarita never considered herself pretty.'

The example in 49b shows that the DO *apne aap ko* 'to herself' is scrambled leftward; however, it is still bound by the antecedent *sariitaa*. Principle-A of the Binding Theory requires anaphors to be in the same governing category as their antecedents and antecedents to c-command the anaphors. In 49b, however, the DO *apne aap ko* 'to herself' is not in a c-command relation with the antecedent *sariitaa* after leftward scrambling takes place. Yet the sentence in 49b is grammatical. It is argued that in this case, for the antecedent to c-command the anaphor and subsequently bind it, the anaphor must reconstruct at LF.

Aoun and Benmamoun (1998) show a similar phenomenon in Arabic (primarily arguing for a PF based account): fronted PPs in Arabic display reconstruction effects. Fronted PPs and scrambled NPs (to A-bar positions) display reconstruction effects in Hindi, too, as shown in the following example:

(50) bacce   ek dusre   ke saath   khel   rahe   the
     children   each other   with   play   PROG   were
     'Children were playing with each other.'

In 50, the PP *ek dusre ke saath* 'with each other' contains a reciprocal (anaphor) *ek dusre* 'each other,' which is bound by the c-commanding subject *bacce* 'children.' This obeys the standard assumptions of Principle-A of the Binding Theory. Principle-A requires that c-commanding antecedents bind anaphors in their governing categories. However, this does not seem to be the case when the PP in 51 is scrambled.

(51) ek duusre   ke saath$_i$ bacce   t$_i$ khel   rahe   the
     each other   with   children   play   PROG   were
     'Children were playing with each other.'

In 51, the PP *ek duusre ke saath* contains an anaphor, and it scrambles where it is not in a c-command relation with its antecedent, *bacce*. However, 51 is still grammatical and does not appear to violate binding conditions on anaphors. The grammaticality of 51 can be explained if we assume that reconstruction takes place (so that the fronted elements can be interpreted in their original position at LF). Thus, in 51, the PP reconstructs back to its original position for the purpose of binding.

Reconstruction may be invoked for the licensing of NPIs, particularly when negation markers do not c-command the NPIs. The potential problem for the licensing of NPIs by the application of this phenomenon is discussed in section 3.6. First of all, reconstruction applies only when an element has moved from its original position. Thus, the process of reconstruction can only rescue cases of NPIs in scrambled clauses, so that they can be put in the c-commanding domain of their negation markers. The second problem with respect to NPI licensing and reconstruction is, once again, the question of the licensing of NPIs in subject position, for in such cases NPIs are not subject to reconstruction.

3.6 Problems with the LF Reconstruction–Based Account of NPI Licensing

There is strong evidence that the process of reconstruction cannot apply to the licensing of NPIs. The crucial evidence, which, as far as I know, is novel, involves the interaction of scrambled NPIs and Binding Theory. If scrambled NPIs reconstruct, they end up violating Principle-C of the Binding Theory.

As we have seen so far, Binding conditions are obeyed at LF. Now let us turn to the following example:

(52) raajiiv-ne kah-aa   ki   [vo   pikcar   jo   sariitaa$_i$–ne lii]$_j$
     rajiv-ERG   say-PERF   that that picture which sarita-ERG   take-PERF

     usko$_i$ pasand   hai   t$_j$
     to her   like   is

'Rajiv said that she likes the pictures that Sarita took.'

The clause *vo pikcar jo sariitaa ne lii* in 52 is scrambled and is adjoined to the lower IP. The following example, 53, shows that the application of reconstruction of 52 at LF results in a violation of Principle-C of the Binding Theory. If reconstruction applies in 52, the sentence ends up violating Principle-C, as the pronoun *usko* 'to her' c-commands its antecedent, *sariitaa*.

(53) * rajiiv-ne kah-aa   ki   usko$_i$ pasand   hai
       rajiv-ERG say-PERF   that to her like   is

       [vo   pikcar   jo   sariitaa$_i$-ne   lii]
       that   picture which sarita-ERG   take-PERF

   * 'Rajiv said that she$_i$ likes the pictures that Sarita$_i$ took.'

Similar observations are noted if we look at the licensing of NPIs. If the licensing of NPIs takes place at LF by providing a c-commanding licensor, then the sentence in 55, below, should be grammatical. Let us first consider the sentence in 54, where the clause *vo koi bhii pikcar jo sariitaa ne lii* is scrambled. The scrambled clause is reconstructed at LF, and the sentence in 55 is ungrammatical on the intended reading, because the pronoun *usko* ends up c-commanding its antecedent, *sariitaa*, violating Binding Principles.

(54) raajiiv-ne kah-aa   ki   [vo koi   bhii pikcar jo   sariitaa$_i$–ne lii]$_j$
     rajiv-ERG say-PERF that that some even picture which sarita-ERG take-PERF

     usko$_i$ pasand   nahiiN   hai   t$_j$
     to her   to like   NEG

'Rajiv said that she does not like any picture that Sarita took.'

(55) * raajiiv-ne kah-aa   ki   usko$_i$ pasand nahiiN hai
     rajiv-ERG   say-PERF   that   to her   like   NEG   is

    [vo   koi   bhii   pikcar   jo   sariitaa$_i$ ne   lii]
    that any   also   picture which   sarita   ERG took

    * 'Rajiv said that she$_i$ does not like any picture that Sarita$_i$ took.'

The example in 55 is ungrammatical on the reading where the NP *sariitaa* is co-referential with the pronoun *usko* in the main clause. It is well formed otherwise. As we see in 55, the scrambled clause reconstructs, then a binding violation occurs. The application of reconstruction at the cost of violating Binding Principles does not seem to be a plausible solution. We can, therefore, say that reconstruction does not take place at all in 54. If so, then the NPI *koi* within the scrambled clause [*vo koi bhii pikcars jo sariitaa ne lii*] remains unlicensed, as it is not within the domain of a c-commanding negative licensor. It follows from the facts of Binding Theory that the scrambled clause does not reconstruct. Hence, the NPI within the scrambled clause is licensed at some level of representation other than LF. In the next section, I propose an analysis of NPI licensing that does not involve any covert movement yet accounts for the licensing of NPIs in Hindi.

4. ANALYSIS

The discussion above demonstrates that the movement of Neg at LF for the licensing of NPIs in Hindi and the alternative LF (reconstruction) approach do not account for the licensing of NPIs in Hindi. The first account (Mahajan 1990a), which involves LF raising of Neg, does not show any proper motivation for the raising of Neg other than to provide a c-commanding licensor. The alternative account, which argues that a c-commanding licensor can be provided by the process of reconstruction, ends up violating Binding Principles. At this point, the NPI licensing remains an unsolved problem, as the negative licensor in Hindi is not in a position from which it can c-command the NPI. At s-structure, Neg is in a position that is lower than the NPI,[2] so that the c-command condition for the licensing of NPIs does not obtain, at least in the cases where NPIs are in subject position.

Thus, we have a paradox. There seems to be no clear account of the licensing of NPIs in Hindi. I, therefore, propose that NPIs are licensed overtly prior to scrambling/movement, in the course of derivation (at s-structure). A clause mate negative licensor must c-command the NPI. However, some indefinites that obtain an NPI interpretation in the presence of a negative licensor can also be licensed long-distance. My analysis is able to account for NPIs in subject position.[3] Let us consider the following example, in 56, the derivation of the simple sentence, where I show that the NPI is licensed at s-structure. The structure in 56b represents 56a.

(56) a. koi   bhii   dillii   *(nahiiN)   aa-yaa   thaa
        someone even   Delhi   NEG   come-PERF   was
        'No one had come to Delhi.'

   b.

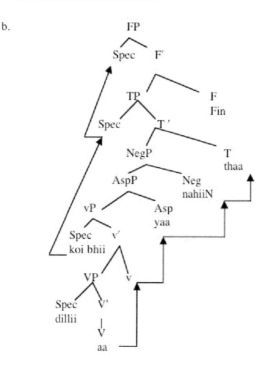

For the purpose of the analysis of NPI licensing, I adopt the VP internal subject hypothesis, as discussed in Chapter Two. Under my analysis, Neg heads its own maximal projection below TP and above AspP. For both the subject NPIs and object NPIs, the negative licensor is in the head of NegP and in a c-commanding relation with the NPI in the Spec of vP. Thus, Neg c-commands and licenses NPIs in any position in the sentence. The negative licensor does not move. Any scrambling operation takes place after the licensing has taken place. This analysis applies also to cases of long-distance licensing of NPIs but does not claim to account for the licensing of NPIs in the absence of a non-negative licensor.

Now let us consider the following sentences, which show the licensing of NPIs in object positions, as in 57a and 58a, and the representation of these sentences, in 57b and 58b:

(57) a. raajiiv ek bhii kitaab nahiiN paRh-taa hai
     rajiv one even book NEG read-HAB is
    'Rajiv does not read any book.'

b.

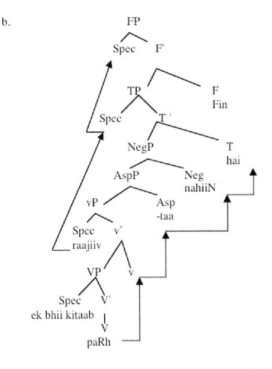

The structure in 57b shows that Neg c-commands the NPI *ek bhii* 'any' in the Spec position (DO) of the VP. This shows that Neg c-commands object NPIs. The fundamental idea of this analysis is that the licensing of NPIs takes place prior to scrambling or movement in the course of a derivation and subsumes the idea that Neg c-commands both the subject and the object positions.

(58) a. raajiiv tum ko ek phuuTii kauRii nahiiN de-gaa
     rajiv you to one broken penny NEG give-FUT
    'Rajiv will not give a red cent to you.'

(58) b.

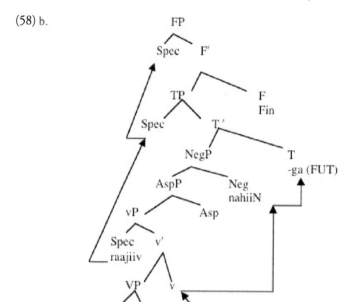

The structure in 58b shows that Neg c-commands the NPI *ek phuuTii kau-Rii,* which is the direct object of the sentence. The licensing of the NPI takes place prior to scrambling; therefore, the Neg in the head of the NegP c-commands both the subject and object positions.

In the following sentence, 59a, and structure, in 59b, I show how NPIs are licensed in cases of scrambling.

(59) a. [kisii   ko   bhii]ᵢ   sariitaa-ne   kah-aa   ki   raajiiv-ne
        someone   to   even   sarita-ERG   say-PERF   that   rajiv-ERG

        t ᵢ nahiiN dekh-aa   thaa
        NEG   see-PERF   was

        'Sarita said that Rajiv had not seen anyone.'

b.

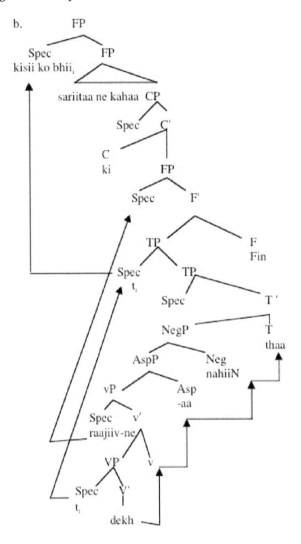

In 59a, the direct object of the subordinate clause is *kisii ko bhii*, which is an NPI and has scrambled to the left and is adjoined to the matrix clause. The NPI originates in the Spec of VP, and we see in 59a that it is not in a position where the negation marker in the matrix clause can c-command and license it, so the sentence should be ungrammatical. However, the sentence is grammatical, which means that the scrambled NPI in the adjoined position in the

matrix clause is licensed. The sentence is good, because the NPI is licensed in
the subordinate clause by the negation in the subordinate clause prior to the
scrambling operation.

Similarly, in 60, the NPI *koi bhii* is within the scrambled clause [*vo koi
bhii pikcar jo sariitaa ne lii*], where it is higher than the Neg and, hence, unlicensed.

(60) a. raajiiv-ne   kah-aa   ki   [vo   koi   bhii   pikcar
       rajiv-ERG   say-PERF   that   that   someone   even   picture

       jo   sariitaa$_i$-ne   lii]$_j$ usko$_i$ pasand   nahiiN   hai   t$_j$
       which   sarita-ERG   take-PERF   to her   like   NEG   is

       'Rajiv said that Sarita does not like any picture that she took.'

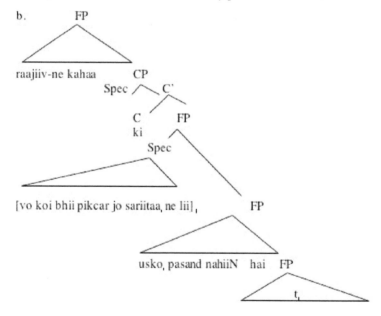

The NPI in 60b is in the scrambled clause [*vo koi bhii pikcar jo sariitaa ne
lii*]. In 60a, it appears to be the case that Neg does not c-command the NPI,
as the Neg is in the lower clause and the NPI is in the higher clause. However, the intended reading of the sentence is grammatical. The grammaticality of the sentence clearly shows that the NPI is licensed. In the scrambled
clause, it is licensed prior to the scrambling operation. Also, I would like to

point out that the scrambled clause does not reconstruct, as it would end up violating Principle-C of the Binding Theory. Reconstruction of the scrambled clause to the base position allows the pronominal to bind its antecedent. Thus, NPIs are in the c-command domain of the negative licensor under my analysis; they are licensed by their negative licensors prior to scrambling. The negative licensor does not move, in order to license the NPIs in scrambled clauses.

4.1 Licensing Conditions on NPIs

We have seen that there are two types of NPIs in Hindi. Some NPIs, such as *ek phuuTii KauRii* 'a broken penny,' *Tas se mas na hona* 'to budge an inch,' *baal na baNkaa karnaa* 'not being able to make a difference,' etc., do not occur in all the contexts where the second type of NPIs—namely *koi bhii* 'anybody,' *kisii bhii* 'anybody,' and *kuch bhii* 'anything'—can occur. In other words, NPIs such as *ek phuuTii KauRii* 'a broken penny,' *Tas se mas na hona* 'to budge an inch,' *baal na baNkaa karnaa* 'not being able to make a difference,' etc., do not occur in the contexts of questions, conditionals, modals, or adversative predicates, whereas the second type of NPIs—*koi bhii* 'anybody,' *kisii bhii* 'anybody,' and *kuch bhii* 'anything'—can occur in those contexts. In the next chapter, I will discuss further the syntactic constraints that are instrumental in isolating NPIs from one another. I refer to NPIs such as *ek phuuTii KauRii* 'a broken penny,' *Tas se mas na hona* 'to budge an inch,' *baal na baNkaa karnaa* 'not being able to make a difference,' etc., as strong NPIs and to NPIs such as *koi bhii* 'anybody,' *kisii bhii* 'anybody,' and *kuch bhii* 'anything' as weak NPIs. One of the major syntactic constraints that distinguishes them from one another is that the first type of NPI requires a very local negative licensor and cannot be licensed long-distance, whereas the second type of NPI can be licensed locally as well as long-distance. However, NPIs of both types are licensed overtly prior to scrambling. In this section, I will formulate their licensing conditions.

First, I will show that strong NPIs are not licensed long-distance, whereas weak NPIs can be licensed long-distance. In 61a and 61c, the NPIs *ek phuuTii KauRii* 'a broken penny' and *Tas se mas na hona* 'to budge an inch' are licensed, as they occur with a clause mate negative licensor, whereas they are not licensed in 61b and 61d in the absence of a clause mate negative licensor, as the ungrammaticality of the examples suggests. In 61b and 61d, the negative licensor *nahiiN* is in the higher clause, and the NPIs are in the lower clause.

(61) a. raajiiv   ek   phuuTii   kauRii   nahiiN   degaa
       rajiv   one   broken   penny   NEG   give-FUT
       'Rajiv will not give a red cent.'

    b. * sariitaa-ne   nahiiN   kahaa   ki
        sarita-ERG   NEG   say-PERF   that

        raajiiv   ek   phuuTii   kauRii   degaa
        rajiv   one   broken   penny   give-FUT

        'Sarita did not say that Rajiv will give a red cent.'

    c. raajiiv   Tas se mas   nahiiN   hogaa
       rajiv   deviate   NEG   be-FUT
       'Rajiv will not budge an inch.'

    d. * sariitaa-ne   nahiiN   kahaa   ki   raajiiv   Tas se mas   hogaa
        sarita-ERG   NEG   say-PERF   that   rajiv   deviate   be-FUT
        'Sarita did not say that Rajiv will budge an inch.'

In 62, on the other hand, the NPIs *koi bhii* 'anybody' and *kisii bhii* 'anybody' are licensed locally as well as long-distance. In 62a and 62c, the negative licensors are locally present to license NPIs, whereas in 62b and 62d, the negative licensors are in the higher clause and the NPIs are in the lower clause; still the negative licensors license the NPIs, as the grammaticality of these sentences suggests.

(62) a. koi   bhii   nahiiN   aa-yaa
       someone   even   NEG   come-PERF
       'No one came.'

    b. sariitaa-ne   nahiiN   kahaa   ki   koi   bhii   aa-yaa
       sarita-ERG   NEG   say-PERF   that   someone   even   come-PERF
       'Sarita did not say that anybody came.'

    c. maiN-ne   kisii   bhii   sTuDeNT   ko   nahiiN   dekh-aa
       I-ERG   some   even   student   to   NEG   see-PERF
       'I did not see any student.'

    d. sariitaa-ne   nahiiN kahaa   ki   maiN-ne   kisii   bhii   sTuDeNT
       sarita-ERG   NEG   say-PERF   that   I-ERG   someone   even   student

       ko   dekh-aa
       to   see-PERF

       'Sarita did not say that I saw any student.'

Having established syntactic differences between the two types of NPIs and also having established that NPIs are licensed overtly, I will formulate the licensing conditions now. All NPIs must be licensed by a c-commanding negative licensor, where c-command is defined as in Reinhart (1976:32): Node A c-commands node B if neither A nor B dominates the other and the first branching node dominating A dominates. This condition alone does not account for why strong NPIs are not licensed long-distance. As we observe in the discussion above, strong NPIs require a local c-commanding negative licensor. Keeping that in mind, one observes that the licensing of NPIs in Hindi requires two conditions: Strong NPIs are licensed by a c-commanding negative licensor within the CP, whereas weak NPIs require only a c-commanding negative licensor.

5. CONCLUSION

This chapter started with a description of NPIs and a detailed discussion of their distribution. On the basis of their distribution, I suggest that there are two groups of NPIs: namely strong NPIs (which strictly require a clause mate c-commanding negative licensor) and weak NPIs (which can be interpreted as NPIs without the presence of a c-commanding negative licensor and are allowed in questions, conditionals, modals, and adversative predicates). I proceeded to discuss the available accounts regarding the licensing of NPIs in other languages (Jackendoff 1969, Lasnik 1975, Ladusaw 1979, Linebarger 1980, Progovac 1994, and Laka 1994), and, while doing so, I showed the inadequacies of such analyses for the account of NPIs in languages such as Hindi. I discussed the problems with the existing analysis of the licensing of NPIs in Hindi (Mahajan 1990a). Finally, I proposed my analysis and showed how NPIs in different positions are licensed overtly prior to scrambling. I showed that NPIs are always licensed overtly in Hindi and that the licensing of NPIs does not involve any covert syntactic operation. There are two different licensing conditions for the two types of NPIs: strong NPIs are licensed by a c-commanding negative licensor within the CP, whereas weak NPIs require a c-commanding negative licensor.

Chapter Five
Syntactic Constraints on NPIs in Hindi

1. INTRODUCTION

In the previous chapter, I proposed an analysis for the licensing of NPIs that dispenses with the LF raising of Neg and dispenses with any covert syntactic operations (specifically reconstruction). I suggest rather that NPIs are licensed overtly prior to scrambling. I also presented a detailed discussion of the distribution of NPIs and showed that two types of NPIs can be clearly demarcated in terms of their syntactic behavior with reference to their licensors.

In this chapter, I discuss the syntactic constraints on the occurrence and licensing of NPIs in Hindi. I also discuss the asymmetries existing between NPIs, and their negative licensors in somewhat greater detail.

Not all NPIs in Hindi are syntactically similar in nature. Their differences in terms of their occurrence and the positioning of their associated negative licensors in a sentence can be explained syntactically. Some NPIs (strong NPIs), such as *ek bhii* 'even one,' *abhii tak* 'so far/until now,' *kabhii* 'never,' *ek phuuTii kauRii* 'a red cent,' *Tas se mas na honaa* 'to budge an inch,' and *baal na baNkaa karnaa* 'not being able to make a difference,' require a strictly local (clause mate) c-commanding negative licensor, whereas others (weak NPIs), such as *koi bhii* 'any' and *kisii bhii* 'any,' do not. The strong NPIs, such as *ek bhii* 'even one,' *abhii tak* 'so far/until now,' *kabhii nahiiN* 'never,' *ek phuuTii kauRii* 'a red cent,' *Tas se mas na honaa* 'to budge an inch,' and *baal na baaNkaa karnaa* 'not being able to make a difference,' additionally obey the locality conditions that usually constrain movement, whereas *koi bhii* 'any' and *kisii bhii* 'any' do not obey any such constraints. The analysis for the licensing of NPIs presented in the previous chapter shows that the condition on the licensing of NPIs in Hindi is having a c-commanding negative licensor. I treat the NPIs that require a clause mate c-commanding negative licensor as strong NPIs and the NPIs that can

be licensed long-distance as weak NPIs. Strong NPIs obey locality constraints, whereas weak NPIs do not. In the following sections, I suggest that
strong NPIs are real NPIs in Hindi and that weak NPIs are quantifiers that
receive NPI interpretation in the presence of a c-commanding negative licensor. As far as the licensing of NPIs in the contexts of questions, conditionals,
modals, and adversative predicates is concerned, only weak NPIs are allowed
in these contexts. This indicates that weak NPIs are really like the free choice
'any' of English.

This chapter is organized as follows: The first section introduces the
nature of the syntactic constraints on NPIs in Hindi (occurrence and licensing). In the second section, I recapitulate the facts regarding the licensing of
NPIs in Hindi for the readers' convenience. The third section presents the
asymmetry between NPIs with reference to the occurrence of their licensors.
The fourth section concludes the chapter.

2. AN OVERVIEW OF NPI LICENSING IN HINDI

As illustrated in the previous chapter, NPIs in Hindi are licensed overtly by a
c-commanding clause mate negative licensor. The following example illustrates this.

(1)   a. ek   bhii   sTuDeNT   nahiiN   aa-yaa
         one   even   student   NEG   come-PERF
         'Not even one student came.'

      b.

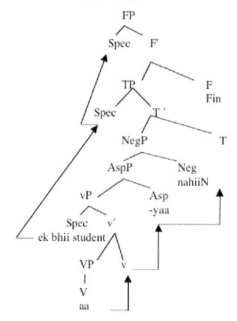

The representation of 1a in 1b clearly shows that under the assumptions of clause structure and the position of negation in clause structure (as discussed in Chapters Two and Three), the negative licensor *nahiiN* c-commands the NPI *ek bhii* 'any/even one' and licenses the NPI overtly.

Now I will briefly recapitulate the distribution of NPIs in Hindi. Recall from the previous chapter that NPIs such as *koi* 'any,' *kisii* 'any,' *ek bhii* 'even one,' *abhii tak* 'so far/until now,' *kabhii* 'never,' *ek phuuTii kauRii* 'a red cent,' *Tas se mas na honaa* 'to budge an inch,' and *baal na baNkaa karnaa* 'not being able to make a difference' require a negative licensor for their legitimate occurrence in a sentence. The absence of such a negative licensor causes those sentences to be ungrammatical. The following sentences illustrate this fact. The sentences in 2 are grammatical, as a negative licensor *nahiiN*—licensing NPIs such as *koi* 'any,' *kisii* 'any,' *ek bhii* 'even one,' *abhii tak* 'so far/until now,' *kabhii* 'never,' *ek phuuTii kauRii* 'a red cent,' *Tas se mas na honaa* 'to budge an inch,' and *baal na baaNkaa karnaa* 'not being able to make a difference'—is present in these sentences.

(2) a. us   kamre   meN   koi   bhii   sTuDeNT   nahiiN   thaa
         that   room   in   some   even   student   NEG   was
      * 'There was no/not even one student in that room.'

     b. maiN-ne   kisii   bhii   sTuDeNT   ko   nahiiN   dekh-aa
        I-ERG   some   even   student   to   NEG   see-PERF
        'I did not see any student.'

     c. us   kamre   meN   ek   bhii   aadmii   nahiiN   thaa
        that   room   in   one   even   man   NEG   was
        'There was not even a single person in that room.'

     d. raajiiv   abhii   tak   nahiiN   aa-yaa
        rajiv   now   until   NEG   come-PERF
        'Rajiv has not come so far.'

     e. maiN   kabhii   nahiiN   jaa-uNgaa
        I   sometime   NEG   go-FUT
        'I will never go.'

     f. maiN   tum   ko   ek   phuuTi   kauRi   nahiiN   duu-Ngaa
        I   you   to   one   broken   penny   NEG   give-FUT
        'I will not give you a red cent.'

     g. vo   Tas   se   mas   nahiiN   huaa
        he   deviate   NEG   happen-PERF
        'He did not budge an inch.'

h. raajiiv tumhaaraa baal   baaNkaa nahiiN kar   sak-egaa
   rajiv   your   hair   disturb NEG   do   MOD-FUT
   'Rajiv cannot harm you.'

However, the absence of clause mate negative licensors in 2 makes these sentences ungrammatical, as shown in 3.

(3) a. * us   kamre   meN   koi   bhii   sTuDeNT   thaa
        that   room   in   some   even   student   was
        * 'There was any student in that room.'

     b. * maiN-ne kisii   bhii   sTuDeNT ko   dekh-aa
        I-ERG   some   even   student to   see-PERF
        * 'I saw any student.'

     c. * us   kamre   meN   ek   bhii   aadmii   thaa
        that   room   in   one   even   man   was
        * 'There was even a single person in that room.'

     d. * raajiiv abhii   tak   aa-yaa
        rajiv   now   until   come-PERF
        * 'Rajiv has come until now.'

     e. * maiN   kabhii   jaa-uNgaa
        I   sometime   go-FUT
        'I will never go.'

     f. * maiN   tum   ko   ek   phuuTi   kauRii   duu-Ngaa
        I   you   to   one   broken   penny   give-FUT
        * 'I will give you a red cent.'

     g. * vo   Tas se mas   huaa
        he   deviate   happen-PERF
        * 'He did budge an inch.'

     h. * raajiiv tumhaaraa baal   baaNkaa kar   sak-egaa
        rajiv   your   hair   disturb do   MOD-FUT
        'Rajiv can harm you.'

The data above in 2 and 3 include some idiomatic expressions, such as *ek phuuTii kauRii* 'a red cent,' *Tas se mas na honaa* 'to budge an inch,' and *baal na baaNkaa karnaa* 'not being able to make a difference.' These phrases are NPIs, as they all require a negative licensor. Recall that only a negative element in pre-verbal position functions as a proper licensor for the NPIs discussed above.

Pre-verbal negation in Hindi is sentential negation, and it occurs immediately preceding the main verb.

3. SYNTACTIC ASYMMETRIES OF NPIS

There are systematic syntactic differences between weak NPIs such as *koi bhii* 'any' and *kisii bhii* 'any,' on the one hand, and strong NPIs such as *ek bhii* 'even one,' *abhii tak* 'so far,' *kabhii* 'never,' *ek phuuTii kauRii* 'a red cent,' *Tas se mas na honaa* 'budge an inch,' and *baal na baaNkaa karnaa* 'not being able to make a difference' on the other hand.

In this section, I show that NPIs such as *ek bhii* 'even one,' *abhii tak* 'so far,' *kabhii* 'never,' *ek phuuTii kauRii* 'a red cent,' *Tas se mas na honaa* 'budge an inch,' and *baal na baaNkaa karnaa* 'not being able to make a difference' are strong (real) NPIs, while *koi bhii* 'any' and *kisii bhii* 'any' are weak NPIs, which are interpreted as NPIs only in the presence of a c-commanding negative licensor. In the absence of a negative licensor—that is, in the context of questions, modals, conditionals, or adversative predicates, weak NPIs are like the English free choice 'any.'

3.1 Local vs. Long-distance Licensing of NPIs

The following data present the systematic contrast between the two types of NPIs; namely the strong NPIs and the weak NPIs. In this section, I show that strong NPIs are not licensed long-distance, whereas weak NPIs can be licensed long-distance. The weak NPIs, such as *koi bhii* 'any' and *kisii bhii* 'any'[1] allow long-distance licensors, as in the sentences in example 4 below.

(4) a. sariitaa-ne   nahiiN   kah-aa   ki   us   kamre   meN koi   bhii
        sarita-ERG   NEG   say-PERF that that room   in   some even

        aadmii   thaa
        person   was

        'Sarita did not say that there was anybody in that room.'

     b. sariitaa-ne   nahiiN   kah-aa   ki   maiN-ne   kisii   bhii laRke ko
        sarita-ERG   NEG   say-PERF that I-ERG   some   even boy   to

        dekh-aa
        see-PERF

        'Sarita did not say that I saw any boy.'

In the sentences in 4, the negative licensor *nahiiN* is in the matrix clause. The negative licensor can license the NPIs *koi bhii* 'any' and *kisii bhii* 'any' in lower clauses. The grammaticality of 4 illustrates this fact. As discussed in Chapter Four, weak NPIs can be licensed locally as well.

On the other hand, NPIs such as *ek bhii* 'even one,' as in 5a, *abhii tak* 'so far/until now,' as in 5b, *kabhii* 'never,' as in 5c, *ek phuuTii kauRii* 'a red cent,' as in 5d, *Tas se mas na honaa* 'budge an inch,' as in 5e, and *baal na baaNkaa karnaa* 'not being able to make a difference,' as in 5f, specifically require a local licensor. The examples in 5 illustrate this fact. The ungrammatical sentences below show that the occurrence of a negative licensor in the matrix clause is not able to license NPIs in the lower clause. As discussed in Chapter Four, these strong NPIs can be licensed if a negative licensor is available in the same clause.

(5) a. */? maiN-nenahiiN kah-aa   ki   sariitaa   ek   bhii laRke se
        I-ERG   NEG   say-PERF that sarita   one   even boy   with

        mil-ii
        meet-PERF

        'I did not say that Sarita met any boy.'

     b. * maiN-ne nahiiN kah-aa   ki   sariitaa abhii tak us laRke se
        I-ERG   NEG   say-PERF that sarita   now   until that boy   with

        mil-ii
        met-PERF

        'I did not say that Sarita met that boy so far.'

     c. * maiN-ne nahiiN kah-aa   ki   sariitaa kabhii   us laRke se
        I-ERG   NEG   say-PERF that sairta   sometime that boy   with

        mil-ii
        meet-PERF

        'I did not say that Sarita never met that boy.'

     d. * raajiiv-ne nahiiN kah-aa   ki   main tum ko ek   phuuTi kauRii
        rajiv-ERG NEG   say-PERF that I   you to one broken penny

        duu-Ngaa
        give-FUT

        'Rajiv did not say that I will give you a red cent.'

e. * raajiiv-ne   nahiiN   kahaa   ki   vo   Tas se mas   huaa
   rajiv-ERG   NEG   say-PERF   that he   deviate   happen-PERF
   'Rajiv did not say that he did not budge an inch.'

f. * raajiiv-ne   nahiiN   kah-aa   ki   ramesh   meraa   baal   baaNkaa   kar
   rajiv-ERG   NEG   say-PERF   that   remesh   my   hair   disturb   do

   sak-egaa
   MOD-FUT

   'Rajiv did not say Ramesh can harm me.'

The sentences in 5 are ungrammatical because the negative licensors are in the matrix clause and the NPIs in the lower clause. In other words, NPIs such as *ek bhii* 'even one,' as in 5a, *abhii tak* 'so far/until now,' as in 5b, *kabhii nahiiN* 'never,' as in 5c, *ek phuuTii kauRii* 'a red cent,' as in 5d, *Tas se mas na honaa* 'budge an inch,' as in 5e, and *baal na baaNkaa karnaa* 'not being able to make a difference,' as in 5f, require a local (clause mate) licensor.

Thus, there exists an asymmetry between the two types of NPIs in Hindi. Before I proceed to derive generalizations from this asymmetry that the NPIs such as *ek bhii* 'even one,' *abhii tak* 'so far/until now,' *kabhii nahiiN* 'never,' *ek phuuTii kauRii* 'a red cent,' *Tas se mas na honaa* 'budge an inch,' and *baal na baaNkaa karnaa* 'not being able to make a difference' are real NPIs while *koi bhii* 'any' and *kisii bhii* 'any' are only interpreted as NPIs in the presence of a c-commanding negative licensor, let us recall the discussions from Laka (1994) and Progovac (1994) from the previous chapter.

To account for examples such as 4, above, Laka (1994) suggests that the negated verbs select for a special type of negative complementizer, as the negative licensor in the matrix clause fails to license the NPI in the embedded clause. Consider the examples in 6 and 7.

(6) a. [That anyone might do anything like that] never occurred to John.
     b. $[_{CP}$ [Neg] COMP $[_{IP} \ldots NPI \ldots]]_i \ldots V Neg \ldots t_i \ldots$

(7) a. Mary does not think that Ann read any books last week.
     b. $\ldots V Neg \ldots [_{CP}$ [Neg] COMP $[_{IP} \ldots NPI \ldots]]$

As we have seen in the previous chapter, as well with reference to Laka (1994), negative licensors in the matrix clause do not license the NPIs in 6 and 7. Laka, therefore, states that the negative licensor in the matrix clause does not license the NPI in the lower clause; rather, the negative COMP selected by the negated verb in the matrix clause licenses the NPI in the lower clause. Her analysis may work for some of the NPIs (specifically weak NPIs) in Hindi, and it explains the following set of examples.

(8) a. sariitaa-ne   nahiiN kahaa   ki   us   kamre meN koi   bhii aadmii
        sarita-ERG   NEG   say-PERF   that that room in some   even person

        thaa
        was

        'Sarita did not say that there was anybody in that room.'

     b. . . . nahiiN (Neg) V . . . [$_{CP}$ [Neg] COMP [$_{IP}$ . . . koi bhii (NPI) . . .]]

     c. sariitaa-ne   nahiiN kah-aa   ki   maiN-ne kisii bhii laRke ko
        sarita-ERG   NEG   say-PERF   that I-ERG   some   even boy   to

        dekh-aa
        see-PERF

        'Sarita did not say that I saw any boy.'

     d. . . . nahiiN (Neg) V . . . [$_{CP}$ [Neg] COMP [$_{IP}$ . . . kisii bhii (NPI) . . .]]

In 8a and 8c, the negated verb *kahaa* selects a negative COMP, as shown in 8b and 8d. Thus, we can say that NPIs in 8a and 8c are licensed by the negative COMP. However, Laka's assumption of a negative COMP does not work for strong NPIs in Hindi. The examples in 9 illustrate this.

(9) a. */? maiN-ne nahiiN kah-aa   ki   sariitaa ek   bhii laRke se
        I-ERG   NEG   say-PERF   that sarita   one   even boy   with

        mil-ii
        meet-PERF

        'I did not say that Sarita met any boy.'

     b. * maiN-ne nahiiN kah-aa   ki   sariitaa abhii tak   us laRke se
        I-ERG   NEG   say-PERF   that sarita   now   until that boy with

        mil-ii
        meet-PERF

        'I did not say that Sarita met that boy so far.'

c. * maiN-ne nahiiN kah-aa   ki   sariitaa kabhii   us   laRke se
    I-ERG   NEG   say-PERF   that   sarita   sometime   that boy   with

    mil-ii
    meet-PERF

    'I did not say that Sarita never met students.'

d. * raajiiv-ne   nahiiN kah-aa   ki   maiN tum ko ek phuuTi kauRii
    rajiv-ERG   NEG   say-PERF   that   I   you   to   one broken   penny

    duu-Ngaa
    give-FUT

    'Rajiv did not say that I will give you a red cent.'

e. * raajiiv-ne   nahiiN   kah-aa   ki   vo   Tas se mas   huaa
    rajiv-ERG   NEG   say-PERF   that   he   deviate   happen-PERF
    'Rajiv did not say that he did not budge an inch.'

f. * raajiiv-ne   nahiiN kah-aa ki   ramesh meraa baal baaNkaa kar
    rajiv-ERG   NEG   said   that   ramesh my   hair disturb   do

    sak-egaa
    MOD-FUT

    'Rajiv did not say that Ramesh can harm me.'

All the examples in 9 have a negated verb in the matrix clause. However, the negative COMP in 9 does not license the NPIs in the lower clause. Clearly, the analysis under which a negated verb selects a negative COMP does not explain the ungrammaticality of the examples in 9.

Now let us turn to Progovac (1994). Recall the discussion of Serbo-Croatian NI-NPIs and I-NPIs. Serbo-Croatian is somewhat parallel to Hindi in expressing a locality restriction (local and long-distance licensing) similar to that which Hindi NPIs show. NI-NPIs occur only in the presence of an overt clause mate negative licensor. Thus, the NI-NPIs of Serbo-Croatian are parallel to the strong NPIs of Hindi. Let us consider the examples below (repeated from the previous chapter).

(10) a. milan   ne   vidi   nista
       Milan   NEG   sees   nothing
       'Milan cannot see anything.'

    b. * milan   vidi   nista
       Milan sees   nothing

    c. * milan ne   tvrdi [da marija poznaje nikio-ga
       Milan NEG sees   that Mary   knows   none
       'Milan does not claim that Mary knows no one.'   (From Progovac 1994)

On the other hand, I-NPIs are also licensed by a negative licensor, but the negative licensor must be in the matrix clause. If they are in the same clause, then the sentence is ungrammatical. In this case, Serbo-Croatian I-NPIs are parallel to the Hindi NPIs *koi bhii* 'anybody' and *kisii bhii* 'anybody' to the extent that these Hindi NPIs can be licensed long-distance as well. Let us consider the following examples, repeated from the last chapter.

(11) a. * milan ne   zna   ista
       Milan NEG knows anything
       'Milan does not know anything.'

    b. milan ne   tvrdi [da marija poznaje iko-ga
      Milan NEG sees   that Mary   knows   none
      'Milan does not claim that Mary knows no one.'   (From Progovac 1994)

Progovac's (1994) approach to the licensing of NPIs is summarized below (also see the previous chapter for details). Along the lines of Generalized Binding of Aoun (1985 and 1986), Progovac argues that NPIs in Serbo-Croatian are anaphoric. To capture the distributional properties of Serbo-Croatian NI-NPIs and I-NPIs, Progovac suggests that NI-NPIs are subject to Principle-A while I-NPIs are subject to both Principle-A and Principle-B. I-NPIs obey restrictions on Principle-B at surface structure and obey the requirements of Principle A at LF. As the negative licensors are not clause mates with I-NPIs at surface structure, I-NPIs move at LF to be bound within the governing category.

Now the long-distance licensing facts of Hindi weak NPIs *koi bhii* 'anybody' and *kisii bhii* 'anybody' can be explained in the spirit of Progovac (1994), as shown in the following examples:

(12) a. sariitaa-ne nahiiN kah-aa   ki   us   kamre meN koi   bhii aadmii
      sarita-ERG NEG   say-PERF that that room in   some even person

      thaa
      was

      'Sarita did not say that there was anybody in that room.'

b. . . . nahiiN (Neg) V . . . [$_{CP}$ COMP [$_{IP}$ . . . koi bhii (NPI) . . .]]

c. sariitaa-ne nahiiN kah-aa   ki maiN-ne kisii bhii laRke ko
   sarita-ERG NEG say-PERF that I-ERG   some even boy   to

   dekh-aa
   see-PERF

   'Sarita did not say that I saw any boy.'

d. . . . nahiiN (Neg) V . . . [$_{CP}$ COMP [$_{IP}$ . . . kisii bhii (NPI) . . .]]

In 12a and 12c, negative licensors are in the matrix clause and NPIs are in the lower clause. Examples 12a and 12c are schematically represented in 12b and 12d, respectively. Following Progovac's assumption, we have to say that the NPIs in 12 move out of the lower clause at LF, and, thus, they are licensed. However, as we have seen in the previous chapter, LF movement of either NPIs or Neg is problematic in Hindi.

(13) a. */? maiN-ne nahiiN kah-aa   ki sariitaa   ek   bhii laRke se
     I-ERG   NEG say-PERF that sarita   one even boy   with

     mil-ii
     meet-PERF

     'I did not say that Sarita met any boy.'

b. * maiN-ne nahiiN kah-aa   ki   sariitaa abhii tak   us   laRke se
   I-ERG   NEG say-PERF that sarita   now   until that boy   with

   mil-ii
   meet-PERF

   'I did not say that Sarita met that boy so far.'

c. * maiN-ne nahiiN kah-aa   ki   sariitaa kabhii   us   laRke se
   I-ERG   NEG say-PERF that sarita   sometime that boy   with

   mil-ii
   meet-PERF

   'I did not say that Sarita never met students.'

d. * raajiiv-ne nahiiN kah-aa   ki   maiN tum ko ek phuuTi kauRii
   rajiv-ERG NEG say-PERF that I   you to one broken penny

   duu-Ngaa
   give-FUT

   'Rajiv did not say that I will give you a red cent.'

e. * raajiiv-ne   nahiiN   kah-aa   ki   vo   Tas se mas   huaa
   rajiv-ERG   NEG   say-PERF   that he   deviate   happen-PERF
   'Rajiv did not say that he did not budge an inch.'

f. * raajiiv-ne   nahiiN   kah-aa   ki   ramesh   meraa   baal   baaNkaa kar
   rajiv-ERG   NEG   say-PERF   that ramesh   my   hair   disturb   do

sakegaa
MOD-FUT

'Rajiv did not say that Ramesh can harm me.'

I will briefly mention here that the LF movement approach to NPI licensing (Mahajan 1990a) does not provide any solution to this asymmetry of NPI licensing found between strong and weak NPIs in Hindi. In Mahajan's analysis, the negative licensor moves obligatorily at LF to provide a c-commanding licensor. However, in this case the negative licensor is already higher than the NPI.

Both types of Hindi NPIs are licensed in light of the analysis presented in the previous chapter, where NPIs are licensed overtly under the notion of c-command by a negative licensor. The strong NPIs are licensed by a c-commanding negative licensor within the CP, and the weak NPIs require only a c-commanding negative licensor.

In all the examples in 14, however, the negative licensor does c-command the NPI, so the elements such as *koi bhii* 'anybody' and *kisii bhii* 'anybody' receive NPI interpretations. Also, 14 shows that weak NPIs require only a c-commanding negative licensor.

(14) a. sariitaa-ne   nahiiN   kah-aa   ki   meghaa   jaantii   hai ki
        sarita-ERG   NEG   say-PERF   that megha   know-HAB   is   that

     us   kamre   meN   koi   bhii   aadmii   thaa
     that   room   in   some   even   person   was

     'Sarita did not say that Megha knows that there was anybody in that room.'

b. . . . nahiiN (Neg) V . . . [$_{CP}$ COMP [$_{IP}$ [$_{CP}$ COMP [$_{IP}$ . . . koi bhii (NPI) . . .]]]]

c. sariitaa-ne   nahiiN   kah-aa   ki   raajiiv   ko   lagt-aa   hai ki
   sarita-ERG   NEG   say-PERF   that rajiv   to   seem-HAB   is   that

   meghaa   jaan-tii   hai ki   maiN-ne   kisii   bhii   laRke   ko   dekh-aa
   megha   know-HAB   is   that I-ERG   some   even   boy   to   see-PERF

   'Sarita did not say that Rajiv thinks that Megha knows that I saw any boy.'

d. . . . nahiiN (Neg) V . . . [CP COMP [IP [CP COMP [IP [CP COMP [IP
. . . kisii bhii (NPI)

. . .]]]]]]

(15) a. * raajiiv-ne koi   bhii film   dekh-ii   aur ghar nahiiN gayaa
        rajiv-ERG   some even film   watch-PERF and home NEG   went
        'Rajiv watched any film and did not go home'

    b. [IP [VP . . . NPI . . .] and [VP . . . neg . . .]]

The examples in 14 show that elements such as *koi bhii* and *kisii bhii* 'anybody' are licensed long-distance and interpreted as NPIs as long as they are
in the domain of a c-commanding negative licensor. In 14a, the negative
licensor is in the matrix clause, whereas the NPI is in the second subordinate
clause. In 14c, the negative licensor is still in the matrix clause, but the NPI
is in the third subordinate clause. In 15, the negative licensor *nahiiN* is in the
tensed clause, but the NPI is in the VP and not the CP phase; hence, it is
ungrammatical. The ungrammaticality of 15 shows that if both the negative
licensor and the NPI are not in the same CP, the sentence is ungrammatical.

Weak NPIs such as *koi bhii* and *kisii bhii* 'anybody' occur in the
absence of a negative licensor in the context of questions, conditionals,
modals, and adversative predicates (Lahiri 1998).

3.1.1 Weak NPIs (koi bhii *and* kisii bhii):

In the context of questions:

(16) a. us   kamre meN koi   bhii sTuDeNT thaa (kyaa)
        that room   in   some even student was   what
        'Was there even one/any student in that room?'

    b. aap-ne   kisii bhii sTuDeNT ko dekh-aa   (kyaa)
        you-ERG some   even student to see-PERF   what
        'Did you see any student?'

In the context of conditionals:

(17) a. (agar) us   kamre meN koi   bhii sTuDeNT aa-taa   hai to
        if   that room   in   some even student come-HAB   is   then

    maiN aapko   bataauNgaa
    I   to you tell-FUT

    'I will let you know if any student comes to that room.'

b. (agar) maiN-ne kisii   bhii sTuDeNT ko dekh-aa   to
   if   I-ERG   some   even student   to see-PERF   then

us   ko piiTuuNgaa
him   to hit-FUT

'If I see any student, I will beat him up.'

In the context of modals:

(18) a. us   kamre meN koi   bhii sTuDeNT baiTh sak-taa   hai
     that   room   in   some   even student   sit   MOD-HAB   is
     'Any student can sit in that room.'

b. maiN kisii bhii sTuDeNT se   mil   sak-taa   huuN
   I   some   even student   with meet MOD-HAB   am
   'I can meet with any student.'

In the context of adversative predicates:

(19) a. mujhe aaScarya hai ki   kal   koi   bhii sTuDeNT aa-yaa
     I-DAT surprise is   that yesterday some   even student   come-PERF
     'I am surprised that any student came yesterday.'

b. mujhe aaScarya hai   ki   kal   maiN-ne kisii bhii
   I-DAT surprise is   that yesterday I-ERG   some   even

sTuDeNT ko dekh-aa
student   to see-PERF

'I am surprised that I saw any student yesterday.'

The examples above, in 16, 17, 18, and 19, clearly show that weak NPIs, such as *koi bhii* 'anybody' and *kisii bhii* 'anybody,' are permitted in the absence of negative licensors in questions, as in 16, conditionals, as in 17, modals, as in 18, and adversative predicates, as in 19.

Now I present some data to show that strong NPIs are not allowed in the above-stated contexts in the absence of negative licensors. Let us consider the following examples:

3.1.2 Strong NPIs:

In the context of questions:

(20) a. ?/* raajiiv abhii tak   aa-yaa   (kyaa)
      rajiv   now   until come-PERF   what
      'Did Rajiv come so far?'

b. * voh tum ko   ek   phuuTi kauRii de-gaa   (kyaa)
   he   you to   one   broken broken give-FUT   what
   'Will he give you a red cent?'

c. ?/* vo Tas   se mas huaa   (kyaa)
     he deviate   happen-PERF what
   'Did he budge an inch?'

d. * raajiiv tumhaaraa baal baaNkaa kar sak-egaa   (kyaa)
   rajiv   your   hair disturb do   MOD-FUT   what
   'Will Rajiv be able to harm you?'

e. * raajiiv kii majaal ki   vo   kuch   bol-egaa   (kyaa)
   rajiv   of   possible that he   something speak-FUT what
   'Is it possible for Rajiv that he could say something?'

In the context of conditionals:

(21) a. * (agar) raajiiv abhii tak   aayaa   to   maiN jaa-taa huuN
       if   rajiv   now   until com-PERF   then I   go-HAB am
     * 'If Rajiv has come so far then I am going.'

b. * (agar) voh tum ko   ek   phuuTi kauRii de-taa   de-taa
   if   he   you to   one   broken penny   give-HAB   is

   to   acchaa hai
   then good   is

   * 'If he gives you a red cent, then its okay.'

c. * (agar) vo   Tas   se mas huaa   to   maiN samajhuuNgaa
   if   he   deviate   happen-PERF then I   believe-FUT
   'If he budges an inch, then I will believe it.'

d. * (agar) raajiiv tumhaaraa baal baaNkaa kar sak-egaa
   if   rajiv   your   hair disturb do   can.FUT

   to   maiN maan jaauuNgaa
   then I   believe

   * 'If Rajiv will be able to harm you, then I will believe it.'

e. * (agar) raajiiv kii majaal ki   vo   kuch   bol-egaa
   if   rajiv   of   possible that he   something speak-FUT

   to   maiN samajhuuNgaa
   then I   believe

   'If it is possible for Rajiv that he could say something, then I will believe it?'

In the context of modals:

(22) a. ?/* us   kamre meN ek   bhii sTuDeNT baiTh sak-taa   hai
          that   room   in   one even student sit is HOD-HAB is
          'Even one student ca sit in that room.'

   b. * raajiiv abhii tak   aa   sak-taa   hai
        rajiv   now   until come   MOD-HAB is
        * 'Rajiv can come so far.'

   c. * voh tum ko   ek phuuTi kauRii de   sak-taa   hai
        he   you to   one broken penny   give   MOD-HAB is
        'He can give you a red cent.'

   d. * vo   Tas   se mas ho sak-taa   hai
        he   deviate   be MOD-HAB is
        'He can budge an inch.'

   e. * raajiiv tumhaaraa baal baaNkaa kar sak-taa   hai
        rajiv   your   hair disturb do MOD-HAB   is
        * 'Rajiv can be able to harm you.'

   f. * raajiiv kii majaal ki   vo kuch   bol   bol   hai
        rajiv   of   possible that he something speak MOD-HAB is
        'It is possible for Rajiv that he can say something.'

In the context of adversative predicates:

(23) a. ?/* mujhe aaScarya hai ki   kal   ek bhii sTuDeNT
            I-DAT surprise is   that yesterday one even student

            aa-yaa
            come-PERF

            'I am surprised that even one/any student came yesterday.'

   b. * mujhe aaScarya hai ki   raajiiv abhii tak   aa-yaa
        I-DAT surprise is that rajiv   now   until come-PER
        'I am surprised that Rajiv came yet.'

   c. * mujhe aaScarya hai ki   us-ne   tum ko   ek   phuuTi kauRii
        I-DAT surprise is   that he-ERG   you to   one broken penny

        di-yaa
        give-PERF

        'I am surprised that he gave a red cent.'

d. * mujhe aaScarya hai ki   vo Tas   se mas huaa
    I-DAT surprise is that he deviate   happen-PERF

    'I am surprised that he was ready to budge an inch.'

e. * mujhe aaScarya hai ki   raajiiv tumhaaraa baal baaNkaa
    I-DAT surprise is that rajiv   your   hair disturb

    kar sak-aa
    do   MOD-PERF

    'I am surprised that Rajiv will be able to harm you.'

f. * mujhe aaScarya hai ki   raajiiv kii majaal ki
    I-DAT surprise is that rajiv   of   possibl that

    vo kuch   bol-egaa
    he something speak-FUT

    'I am surprised that it is possible for Rajiv that he could say something.'

The data above in 20, 21, 22, and 23 show that strong NPIs are not permitted in the absence of a negative licensor in the context of questions, as in 20, conditionals, as in 21, modals, as in 22, or adversative predicates, as in 23. The ungrammaticality of these examples clearly demonstrates this fact. Note that strong NPIs are permitted in the presence of a negative licensor, as shown in the previous chapter.

Let us revisit the analyses in Laka (1994) and Progovac (1994) again. Laka assumes the selection of a negative COMP primarily to provide a syntactic account for the fact that NPIs are licensed in sentential subjects, where the NPI, as she claims, is not c-commanded by the negative licensor. According to Laka, and as Uribe-Echevarria (1994) notes, such an assumption also accounts for the licensing of NPIs in adversative predicates. On the other hand, Progovac appeals to the presence of an operator in CP for the licensing of NPIs in all the contexts mentioned above (questions, conditionals, modals, and adversative predicates). With particular reference to adversative predicates and on the basis of the following examples, Progovac mentions that adversative verbs are not polarity licensors. Consider the example below:

(24) a.   * John doubts anything.
    b.   * John denied anything.
    c.   John doubts that Mary ate anything.

    d.   John denied that he had eaten anything.

    e.   [IP . . . adversative V [CP OP [IP . . . NPI . . .]]]

Adversative verbs such as *doubt* and *deny* do not license polarity items when polarity items appear as the complements of these verbs. Note that the NPIs are c-commanded by the adversative verbs. However, the NPIs are licensed if they occur in a clausal complement, shown in 24c and 24d. On the basis of the contrast in 24c and 24d, Progovac assumes the presence of an operator in CP, as in 24e, that licenses these NPIs.

    The basic assumption of both analyses does not account for the ungrammaticality of examples in which Hindi strong NPIs are not licensed in adversative predicates, in particular, and in other contexts, such as questions, modals, and conditionals. I rather suggest that the distinction between the two types of NPIs follow from the licensing conditions on them where strong NPIs require a c-commanding negative licensor within the CP and weak NPIs are quantifiers that receive an NPI interpretation in the presence of a c-commanding negative licensor. They are similar to the English free choice 'any.'

    In the following section, 3.2, I discuss the locality constraints on NPI licensing. The following discussion further substantiates the claim that strong NPIs require a clause mate negative licensor whereas weak NPIs are only interpreted as NPIs in the presence of an overt c-commanding negative licensor. I discuss the syntactic island constraints on the two different types of NPIs in the next section as well.

3.2 Island Constraints and NPI Licensing

It is possible to find further differences between weak and strong NPIs in Hindi. The weak NPIs such as *koi bhii* 'any' and *kisii bhii* 'any' can be licensed across syntactic islands. That is to say they violate the island conditions that usually constrain movement. On the other hand, strong NPIs such as *ek bhii* 'even one,' *abhii tak* 'so far/until now,' *kabhii* 'never,' *ek phuuTii kauRii* 'a red cent,' *Tas se mas na honaa* 'budge an inch,' and *baal na baaNkaa karnaa* 'not being able to make a difference' never violate island constraints. Strong NPIs cannot be licensed across syntactic islands. First, I here explore the validity of the claim with respect to Adjunct Islands and later with the Complex NP Constraint (CNPC). Adjuncts and Complex NPs are syntactic islands.

3.2.1 NPIs within Adjunct Islands

The weak NPIs *koi bhii* 'any,' as in 25a, and *kisii bhii* 'any,' as in 25b, are located within adjunct clauses, whereas their negative licensors are located in the main clause outside the island. In 25, the grammaticality of both the sentences shows that weak NPIs are licensed across an adjunct island.

(25) a. raajiiv [koi   bhii baat karne   ke liye] nahiiN aa-yaa   hai
        rajiv some even talk in order to do for NEG   come-PERF is
        'Rajiv did not come to talk about anything.'

   b. raajiiv [kisii   ke bhii ghar jaane   ke liye] nahiiN aa-yaa
        rajiv somebody of even house in order to go for NEG   come-PERF
        'Rajiv did not come to go to anybody's house.'

On the other hand, strong NPIs cannot be licensed across adjunct islands. In other words, they obey locality conditions. Let us consider the validity of this claim in the following examples. The strong NPIs *ek bhii* 'even one,' as in 26a, *abhii tak* 'so far/until now,' as in 26b, *kabhii* 'never,' as in 26c, *ek phuuTii kauRii* 'a red cent,' as in 26d), *Tas se mas na honaa* 'budge an inch,' as in 26e, and *baal na baaNkaa karnaa* 'not being able to make a difference,' as in 26f, are in sentential subjects, whereas their negative licensors are in the main clause. The negative licensors are not able to license NPIs across the sentential subjects in the following sentences:

(26) a. * [ki ek   bhii aadmii aa-yegaa]   bataayaa   nahiiN gayaa   thaa
          that one even person come-FUT tell-PERF NEG   go-PASS   was
          'That nobody will turn up was not told.'

   b. * [ki raajiiv abhii tak   Ph.D. khatam kar paa-yegaa] soc-aa
          that rajiv now   until Ph.D. finish do-MOD-FUT   think-PERF

        nahiiN gayaa   thaa
        NEG   go-PASS   was

        'That Rajiv will finish Ph.D. until now was not thought.'

   c. * [ki raajiiv kabhii   mere ghar aa-yaa]   buraa nahiiN lag-aa
          that rajiv sometime my   home come-PERF bad   NEG   feel-PERF
          'That Rajiv never came to my house did not feel bad.'

   d. * [ki rajiiv ko ghar se   ek phuuTii kauRii mil-ii]   aaScaryajanak
          that rajiv to home from one broken penny get-PERF surprising

        nahiiN thaa
        NEG   was

        'That Rajiv received a red cent from home was not surprising.'

e. * [ki   raajiiv Tas se mas huaa]   aaScaryajanak nahiiN thaa
   that rajiv   deviate   happen-PERF surprising   NEG   was
   'That Rajiv budged an inch was not surprising.'

The strong NPIs are inside adjunct islands in 26. The negative licensors, however, are in the main clauses. Thus, it is clear from the above examples that the negative licensors do not license NPIs across adjunct islands.

3.2.2 NPIs within Complex NPs

Now let us have a look at the NPIs in complex NPs. As mentioned above, the weak NPIs *koi bhii* 'any' and *kisii bhii* 'any' behave similarly with respect to the Complex NP Constraint. They are licensed across complex NPs. In other words, they violate the island constraints. In 27, below, the weak NPIs *koi bhii* 'any,' in 27a, and *kisii bhii* 'any,' in 27b, are inside complex NPs, whereas their respective negative licensors are in the main clauses. The two NPIs in 27a and 27b are licensed across the syntactic islands, as the grammaticality of both sentences below indicates.

(27) a. raajiiv-ne [uskii maaN-ne   jo   koi   bhii baat kah-ii   thii] vo
       rajiv-ERG his   mother-ERG that some even thing tell-PERF was   that

   nahiiN man-ii
   NEG   obey-PERF

   'Rajiv did not obey anything that his mother told him.'

   b. raajiiv [un   aadmioN se   jis   kisii-ne   bhii bhaaShn di-yaa]
      rajiv   those people with which any-ERG even speech give-PERF

   nahiiN mil-aa
   NEG   meet-PERF

   'Rajiv did not meet anybody who gave speeches.'

   Contrary to the behavior of weak NPIs, strong NPIs obey the Complex NP Constraint. The ungrammaticality of the following examples suggests that strong NPIs are not licensed in Complex NPs in the absence of a clause mate (local) negative licensor. In 28, the NPIs are in Complex NPs and the negative licensors are outside the complex NPs. Let us consider the examples in 28:

(28) a. * [vo aadmii jis-ne   ek   bhii kitaab likh-ii]   dilli   meN nahiiN
       that person who-ERG one even book write-PERF delhi in   NEG

       rah-taa
       live-HAB

       'The person who wrote even one book does not live in Delhi.'

    b. * mera   dost   [raajiiv   jo   abhii   tak   aa-yaa]   dilli   meN
       my   friend   rajiv   who   now   until   come-PERF delhi   in

       nahiiN   rah-taa
       NEG   live-HAB

       'My friend Rajiv who has come so far does not live in Delhi.'

    c. * [vo aadmii jis-ne   kabhii   kitaab likh-ii]   dilli   meN
       that person who-ERG sometime book write-PERF delhi   in

       nahiiN   rah-taa
       NEG   live-HAB

       'The person who never wrote a book does not live in Delhi.'

    d. * raajiiv ke pitaajii [jinhoN-ne raajiiv ko ek   phuuTii kauRii dii]
       rajiv   of father   who-ERG   rajiv   to one broken   penny give-PERF

       dilli   meN nahiiN rah-te
       delhi   in   NEG   live-HAB

     * 'Rajiv's father who gave Rajiv a red cent does not live in Delhi.'

    e. * [vo aadmii jis   ko raajiiv Tas se mas kar paa-yaa] dilli   meN nahiiN
       that person who to rajiv deviate   do   got   delhi in   NEG

       rah-taa
       lives

     * 'The person who Rajiv could convince to budge an inch does not live in
       Delhi.'

f. * [vo aadmii jis   kaa raajiiv baal baaNkaa kar paa-yaa]   dilli
      that person who of   rajiv   hair disturb   do   MOD-PERF delhi

meN nahiiN rah-taa
in   NEG   live-HAB

'The person who Rajiv could harm does not live in Delhi.'

The grammaticality of the examples in 27 and the ungrammaticality of the examples in 28 clearly demonstrate the systematic behavior of weak NPIs, on the one hand, and of strong NPIs on the other hand, with respect to island constraints. In 29, I show that if there is a negative licensor present in the complex NP, the sentence turns out to be grammatical.

(29) a. [vo   aadmii jis-ne   ek   bhii kitaab nahiiN likh-ii] dilli   meN
        that person who-ERG one even book   NEG   wrote   delhi   in

rah-taa   hai
live-HAB live-HAB

'The person who did not write even one book lives in Delhi.'

  b. raajiiv ke   pitaajii [jinhoN-ne raajiiv ko   ek   phuuTii kauRii nahiiN
      rajiv   of   father   who-ERG   rajiv   to   one broken penny   NEG

dii]   dilli   meN rah-te   haiN
give   delhi   in   live-HAB is

'Rajiv's father who did not give Rajiv a red cent lives in Delhi.'

Thus, weak NPIs do not obey island constraints, whereas strong NPIs do not violate them.

Hindi NPIs are licensed overtly by a c-commanding negative licensor. This explains why the NPIs in adjunct islands, as in 26, and in Complex NPs, as in 28, are not licensed. NPIs are not licensed when this requirement is not met. The NPIs that are licensed long-distance, within adjunct islands and within complex NPs, are weak NPIs, which are similar to the English free choice 'any,' and they receive NPI interpretation in the presence of a c-commanding negative licensor.

In the following section, I discuss a potential counterexample to my analysis of NPI licensing.

3.3 A Potential Counterexample

The discussion in the previous sections suggests that there are two types of
NPIs in Hindi: strong NPIs and weak NPIs. Strong NPIs require a clause
mate c-commanding negative licensor, whereas weak NPIs are quantifiers
and receive NPI interpretation only in the presence of a c-commanding negative licensor.

There appears to be a potential counterexample to my claim that NPIs
are licensed by a c-commanding clause mate negative licensor. Let us consider the following examples:

(30) a. raajiiv-ne   sariitaa ko   [dillii   nahiiN   jaane]   ko   kah-aa
        rajiv-ERG   sarita   to   delhi   NEG   go-INF   to   say-PERF
        'Rajiv told Sarita not to go to Delhi.'

     b. raajiiv-ne kisii bhii laRke ko dillii   nahiiN jaane   ko kah-aa
        rajiv-ERG some even boy   to delhi   NEG   go-INF   to say-PERF
        'Rajiv did not tell any of the boys to go to Delhi.'

     c. ek   bhii   laRkaa dillii   nahiiN   jaanaa   caah-taa
        one   even   boy   delhi   NEG   go-INF   want-HAB
        'None of the boys wants to go to Delhi.'

     d. raajiiv-ne sariitaa ko ek   phuuTii kauRii nahiiN dene   ko kah-aa
        rajiv-ERG sarita   to one broken penny NEG   give-INF to say-PERF
        'Rajiv told Sarita not to give a red cent.'

In 30a, negation does not contain the entire sentence in its scope. This is
because negation is in the infinitival clause. Now consider the examples in
30b, 30c, and 30d. In these sentences, the negation markers in the infinitival clauses license the NPIs *kisii bhii,* as in 30b, *ek bhii,* as in 30c, and *ek
phuuTii kauRii,* as in 30d. In the previous section the asymmetry between
weak and strong NPIs was observed. We saw that strong NPIs require a
clause mate c-commanding negative licensor. In 30c and 30d, there are
strong NPIs. This seems to pose a problem for the licensing condition I propose (NPIs in Hindi are licensed by a clause mate c-commanding negative
licensor).

I argue that the potential problem that we find in the example in 30 is
not a counterexample to the claim that NPIs in Hindi require a clause mate
c-commanding negative licensor for their licensing. The licensing of NPIs in

30 is predicted in the analysis argued in the previous chapter. Consider the explanation below.

Recall the structure of light verbs, the position of negation in the light verb construction, and the licensing of NPIs in light verb construction.

(31) a. raajiiv aufis   saaf   nahiiN kart-aa
         rajiv   office   clean NEG   do-HAB
         'Rajiv does not clean office.'

b.

The light verb (N-/A-NEG-V) in 31a, represented structurally in 31b, shows that the V *kar* 'do' moves to v and then v moves to the right of Neg to obtain the standard word order (Neg+V). Now consider the second option for light verbs (Neg-N-/Adj-V), as shown in 32a and represented in 32b.

(32) a. raajiiv   aufis   nahiiN   saaf   kar-taa
       rajiv   office   NEG   clean   do-HAB
       'Rajiv does not clean office.'

b.

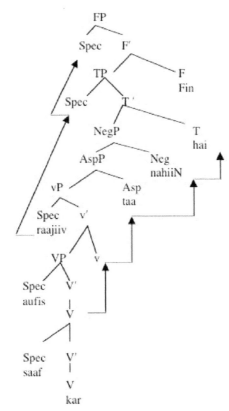

In this case (Neg-N-/Adj-V), the sequence of (Adj+V) forms a compound by an optional movement and moves to v.[2] From there, v further moves to the right of Neg for the word order (Neg-N-/Adj-V)). In both cases, 31 and 32, negation is sentential negation.

Now let us consider the following examples of NPI licensing in the context of light verbs:

(33) a. ek   bhii   laRkaa   aufis   nahiiN   saaf   kar-taa
       one   even   boy   office   NEG   clean   do-HAB
       'None of the boys cleans the office.'

b. ek   bhii   laRkaa   aufis   saaf   nahiiN   kar-taa
       one   even   boy   office   clean   NEG   do-HAB
       'None of the boys cleans the office.'

In 33, the negation *nahiiN* licenses the NPI *ek bhii* in both sentences, as the grammaticality of the sentences shows.

Now we turn to the licensing of NPIs in cases where negation appears to be in infinitival clauses.

(34) a. ek   bhii laRkaa dillii   nahiiN jaanaa   caah-taa
        one   even boy   delhi   NEG   go-INF   want-HAB
        'None of the boys wants to go to Delhi.'

   b. raajiiv-ne sariitaa ko ek   phuuTii kauRii nahiiN dene   ko kah-aa
      rajiv-ERG   sarita   to one broken   penny   NEG   give-INF to say-PERF
      'Rajiv told Sarita not to give a red cent.'

I suggest that the infinitives *jaanaa* in 34a and *denaa* in 34b are nominal in nature. Particularly, the postposition following the infinitive in 34b indicates that the infinitive in this example is nominal, as postpositions follow only nominal elements. These infinitives are in the Spec position of the VP, and they move with the verb to the right of the negation marker in the clause structure. Let us consider the structure in 35, which represents the sentence in 34a.

(35)

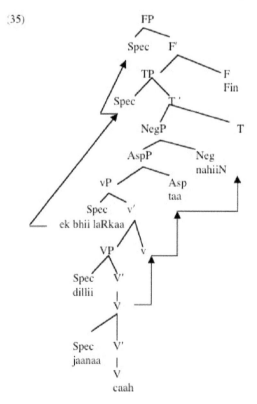

Here the negation is in a c-commanding position, and it is also clause mate to the NPI *ek bhii*. Hence, the NPI is predicted to be licensed under this analysis. In other words, what appears to be a counterexample to my claim that NPIs in Hindi require a c-commanding negative licensor is not really a counterexample.

4. CONCLUSION

In this chapter, I show that there are two types of NPIs in Hindi: strong NPIs such as *ek bhii* 'even one,' *abhii tak* 'so far/until now,' *kabhii* 'never,' *ek phuuTii kauRii* 'a red cent,' *Tas se mas na honaa* 'budge an inch,' and *baal na baaNkaa karnaa* 'not being able to make a difference,' etc., and weak NPIs such as *koi bhii* 'any' and *kisii bhii* 'any.' Strong NPIs are real NPIs, and weak NPIs are quantifiers and receive an NPI interpretation in the presence of a c-commanding negative licensor. There are systematic syntactic constraints governing the differences between these two types of NPIs. The weak NPIs can be licensed locally or by a long-distance licensor; they can also be licensed by a negative licensor from outside a syntactic island. I discuss that in the absence of a negative licensor, weak NPIs are similar to the free choice 'any' of English in the sense of Dayal (1998). However, the strong NPIs specifically require a local licensor and cannot be licensed across a syntactic island. I have shown that NPI licensing in Hindi requires a c-commanding negative licensor.

Notes

NOTES TO CHAPTER ONE

1. The sentence in 8d is ungrammatical only in the intended reading. It is grammatical when the reading is that someone is giving another person a red-colored penny.

NOTES TO CHAPTER TWO

1. In some cases the Relative Clause follows the head noun as well.
2. The example in 13b is not ungrammatical. Rather, it is simply not the canonical order. This is an instance of leftward scrambling.
3. Proper nouns and pronouns differ with regard to Nominative Case marking. That is to say, proper nouns, whether in the Nominative Case position or in the Accusative Case position, are not sensitive to overt case marking. However, pronouns are sensitive to this system. In nominative and Accusative Case positions, pronouns have different forms. Let us look at the following examples. In 1, *vah* 'he' is the Nominative form of the third person singular pronoun, and it is in the subject position, hence grammatical; whereas in 2, the pronoun *vah* 'he' is in the Accusative Case position, hence ungrammatical.

    (1) vah   aam   khaa-taa   hai
          he-IIISG-MASC mango eat-HAB-IIISG-MASC is
          'He eats a mango.'

    (2) * raajiiv   vah   ka dost hai
          rajiv-IIISG-MASC rajiv-IIISG-MASC of friend is
          'Rajiv is his friend.'

4. The marker *ko* is the Dative Case marker as well. I will discuss *ko* as a Dative Case marker in section 3.4.1.4.
5. Thanks to Rakesh Bhatt for pointing this out to me.

6. The subject of a transitive verb is marked with a Case called Ergative. In Ergative languages, the subject of an intransitive verb and the object of a transitive verb are both marked with a Case called Absolutive. Ergative languages are also known as Ergative-Absolutive languages. The other pattern found in languages is Nominative-Accusative. Hindi has both patterns.

7. Hindi verbs carry Aspect and Tense markers, and they agree with the subject in terms of Number, Gender, and Person.

> (3) raajiiv   aam   khaa-taa   hai
>   rajiv-IIISG-MASC mango eat-HAB-IIISG-MASC is
>   'Rajiv eats a mango.'

> (4) sariitaa   aam   nahiiN khaa-tii
>   sarita-IIISG-FEM mango NEG   eat-HAB-IIISG-FEM
>   'Sarita does not eat mango.'

> (5) sariitaa aam   nahiiN khaa rahii   hai
>   sarita   mango NEG   eat   PROG-FEM is
>   'Sarita is not eating mango.'

In the examples above, the subjects *raajiiv* and *sariitaa* are third person singular masculine and feminine, respectively, and they agree with the verbs carrying masculine and feminine morphology. They agree in Number, Person, and Gender. The elements in the verbs *khaataa* and *khaatii*, and *rah* in 5, indicate Imperfect, or Habitual and Progressive Aspect (Kachru 1980). The markers *aa* and *ii* indicate Gender. This is the basic morphological representation of Hindi finite verbs.

8. Some Ergative languages show split-ergativity, where Ergative patterns are conditioned by some part of the grammatical context (typically the persons of the verb arguments, or the Tense/Aspect of the verb). In Hindi, the Ergative (Ergative-Absolutive) construction is allowed in the Past Tense and Perfective Aspect but Accusative (Nominative-Accusative) in the Present Tense (Comrie (1978). In Dyirbal, pronouns are morphologically Nominative-Accusative when the subject is first or second person, but Ergative when the subject is a third person (Dixon 1994).

9. Some of the pronouns change their form if followed by a postposition or a case marker *ko*. Take the following, for example:

> (6) maiN + ko   mujh ko

> (7) vah   + ko   us ko

> (8) kaun + ko   kis ko

10. The present tense marker has a different form for the first person singular *maiN* 'I' and the second person singular and plural, both *tum* 'you.' The Present Tense marker for the first person singular, *maiN* 'I,' is *huuN* 'am,' and the Present Tense marker for the second person singular and plural, *tum* 'you,' is *ho* 'are.' Let us consider the following examples:

(9) main   yahaaN   huuN
     I   here   am
     'I am here.'

(10) tum   kahaaN   ho
     you (SG)   where   are
     'Where are you?'

(11) tum   log   kahaaN   ho
     you   people (PL)   where   are
     'Where are you?'

11. The light verbs with *karnaa* are considered to be transitive, as the subject takes an Ergative Case marker, *ne,* in the Perfect Aspect. The light verbs with *honaa* are intransitive, and therefore the subject does not take the Ergative Case marker *ne* in the Perfect Aspect.

(12) sariitaa-ne   shaadii   kii
     sarita-ERG   marriage   do-PERF
     'Sarita got married.'

(13) raajiiv-Θ   khush   hu-aa
     rajiv-ERG   happy   become-PERF
     'Rajiv was happy.'

12. Yoon (1994) argues that the verbs are inserted in the syntax in their bare, uninflected form and that the syntax builds the inflection contra the checking theory. He also argues that the affixes combine with the root by phrasal affixation, a process that does not involve verb raising in languages such as Korean. This idea needs to be investigated for Hindi. I point this out here to suggest it as a topic for further research.

13. Srivastav (1994) argues that as far as the interaction between scrambling and binding is concerned, scrambling targets only A-bar positions. Srivastav challenges Mahajan's (1994) position and argues that the pre-subject position for scrambling is not an argument position.

(14) a. * apne aap$_i$-ne   mohan$_i$ ko   maaraa
          self-ERG   Mohan   to   beat-PERF
          'Self beat Mohan.'

b.   * mohan$_i$ ko   apne aap$_i$ ne   maaraa

In example 11a we find a reflexive in a subject position and its antecedent in a pre-scrambled position. The scrambling of the antecedent (DO) in a pre-subject position does not change the binding possibilities. Srivastav argues that Mahajan's judgment about the example in 80b is not accepted by a large number of native speakers. Thus, the ungrammaticality of 11b is expected and provides clear evidence that the pre-subject position for scrambling is not an argument position but rather an A-bar position.

NOTES TO CHAPTER THREE

1. There are two variants of the emphatic particle *hiiN* 'only.' They are *hiiN* and *hii*. In modern Hindi, they occur in free variation. There does not seem to be any restriction on the occurrence of the two variants.
2. When the negative marker follows a constituent, the scope of the negative marker is only on the constituent that it follows. In such a situation, the phenomenon is commonly known as "constituent negation." I will discuss this phenomenon in section 4.2 and show how it is different from sentential negation.
3. Here is a brief note on the verb *honaa* 'be' in Hindi. The marker *huuN* occurs only with the first person singular subject, as in 2a above. Similarly, the marker *ho* occurs only with the second person *tum* (both singular and plural), as in 2c above. In the rest of the cases, the morphology of the verb *honaa* 'be' is as follows: *hai*: singular; and *haiN*: plural. They do not display gender agreement. In other words, they do not agree with the subject in terms of gender.
4. This restriction appears to be a result of the morphology of the negation marker *nahiiN*. It is highly likely that the negative marker *nahiiN* is a combination of *na* and the present tense marker *hai*. However, there is no evidence in support of this hypothesis, just as there is no evidence to support the hypothesis that the negation marker *nahiiN* is derived from the combination of the negation marker *na* and the emphatic particle *hii*.
5. The use of the negative marker *mat* is certainly restricted to the imperative and subjunctive sentences. However, in the case of the formal form, i.e. *aap,* some speakers prefer to use *nahiiN*. Some native speakers assert that the negative marker *mat* sound very strong. There seems to be some kind of pragmatic constraint on the use of *nahiiN,* as opposed to *mat,* such that some native speakers do not prefer to use a strong negative marker with the second person formal pronoun *aap*.
6. The modal verb construction (v+Modal) is also different from serial verb construction (v+v) in the sense that while Modal verb constructions do not permit imperative constructions, they can be negated. On the other hand,

serial verb constructions do allow imperative constructions but cannot be negated.

7. At this point, I do not have an explanation for why the verb occurs to the right of the Neg in sentential negation, whereas other heads appears to the left.

8. For the purpose of this analysis, I assume that the Mood and Modal projections are lower than TP and NegP. Following Cinque (1999), we could locate Mood and Modality higher than Tense, which would require slight modification of the structure. Such modification would not impact the main claim about the licensing of NPIs in Hindi.

9. Many studies (Horn 1978 and1989, Ladusaw 1979, Progovac 1994, and others) have shown that sentences get negative interpretations in the absence of an overt negation marker. They also argue that the absence of overt negation licenses negative polarity. Hindi also displays this phenomenon of negating a sentence in the absence of an overt negative marker. I will mention three such ways of negating a sentence: counterfactual mood, lexical elements such as *ThoRe hii,* and questions. Let us consider the following examples:

Counterfactual Mood:

(1)   aap   aate   to   maiN   jaroor   bataa-taa
        you   came   then   I   certainly   tell-HAB
        'I will not tell you.'
        Lit: 'I must have told you if you came.'

Lexical item *ThoRe hii:*

(2)   maiN-ne   ThoRe   hii   kah-aa
        I-ERG   just   EMPH   say-PERF
        'I did not say.'
        Lit: 'It's not me who said.'

Questions:

(3)   a. maiN-ne   kab   kah-aa
           I-ERG   when   say-PERF
           'I did not say.'
           Lit: 'When did I say?'

        b. main   kyoN   kah-uuNgaa
           I   when   say-FUT
           'I will not say.'
           Lit: 'Why would I say?'

The examples mentioned above display contexts where a negative interpretation of a sentence is obtained. In 1, the negative interpretation obtains in counterfactual mood. It is worth mentioning here that counterfactual mood always has a negative interpretation. The example in 2 shows the sentence obtaining a negative interpretation in the presence of the lexical item *ThoRe hii*, which also always gives negative interpretation to the sentence. Finally, questions, though only sometimes, allow negative interpretation as well, as in 3.

NOTES TO CHAPTER FOUR

1. The elements *koi* 'any' and *kisii* 'any' (without the emphatic particle *bhii)* are also interpreted as NPIs in the presence of a negative licensor. However, they have other functions, too. Following Li (1992), I argue in favor of the analysis that such elements are quantifiers, as they are interpreted as indefinites in the absence of a negative licensor. I discuss this phenomenon in the next chapter.

    (1) kal   koi   aa-yaa   thaa
        yesterday   someone   come-PERF   was
        'Somebody came yesterday.'

2. I would like to make it clear here how Neg is assumed to be lower than NPIs in subject position. If the subject originates at the spec of IP position and Neg is below I or under TP, Neg is clearly below the subject and thus does not c-command NPI in the subject position (Spec of IP). In available accounts of NPI licensing (e.g. Mahajan 1990a), the movement of the subject to AgrP is assumed to take place first, and then the question of NPI licensing is addressed. Thus, in either case an asymmetry remains between NPIs in subject position and Neg, and therefore Neg does not c-command NPIs in subject position.
3. This analysis raises the question: why is an NPI in subject position in languages such as English not permitted, as in (2)?

    (2) * Anybody did not come.

    According to the assumptions of the proposed analysis—that the subject NP is in the Spec position of vP and Neg c-commands an NP in such a position— the NPI in the subject position in English should be licensed. A quick answer to this question is that subjects in Hindi and English originate at two different positions in the derivation. In Hindi, subjects originates in the Spec of vP position, whereas in English they originate at the Spec of FP. Neg does not move in either case. Hence, English does not permit NPIs in subject position.

NOTES TO CHAPTER FIVE

1. Consider the following discussion regarding the syntactic distribution of the two NPIs *koi* 'any' and *kisii* 'any.' The NPI *koi* always occurs in subject

position, as in 1, whereas the NPI *kisii* occurs in object position, as in 3. As shown in the example in 2, *kisii* never occurs in Nominative subject position, and, as shown in the example in 4, *koi* never occurs in indirect object position.

(1) kal   koi   nahiiN   aa-yaa
     yesterday   someone   NEG   come-PERF
     'Nobody came yesterday.'

(2) * kisii   student   nahiiN   aa-yaa
       someone   student   NEG   come-PERF
     'No student came.'

(3) tum-ne   kisii   student   ko   dekh-aa
     you-ERG   some   student   to   see-PERF
     'Did you see any student?'

(4) * tum-ne   koi   student   ko   dekh-aa
       you-ERG   some   student   to   see-PERF
     'Did you see any student?'

This calls for an explanation. Interestingly, the NPI *kisii* is the oblique form of the NPI *koi*. We get the NPI *kisii* whenever the NPI *koi* is followed by a postposition. This is the reason why the NPI *kisii* does not occur in subject position. When this element is followed by a postposition, it becomes an oblique NP. Oblique NPs do not appear in syntactic subject positions. The conclusion that follows from the above observation is that Ergative and Dative subjects, in Hindi and in many other languages, may not be syntactic subjects. In light of the discussion presented in this chapter, ergative and dative subjects in Hindi (and in many other languages) require a fresh treatment. Thus, the NPI *kisii* is (*koi*+postposition). As a modifier of an NP in the absence of a postposition, *koi* may occur in object position, as in 5.

(5) tum-ne   koi   kitaab   paRh-ii
     you-ERG   some   book   read-PERF
     'Did you read any book?'

This has a two-fold explanation. First, the postposition in 5 is not required after the NP *book,* as it is not a specific noun; hence, it does not change the NP into oblique Case and remains in Nominative Case. Second, the sentence in 5 has a question interpretation.

2. The formation of a compound by N/A and verb in the context of a negative marker is discussed in Chapter Three.

References

Abbi, A. 1994. Semantic universals in Indian languages. Shimla: Indian Institute of Advanced Study.

Aoun, J. 1985. A grammar of anaphora. Cambridge, MA: MIT Press.

Aoun, J. 1986. Generalized binding. Dordrecht, Netherlands: Foris.

Aoun, J., and E. Benmamoun. 1998. Minimality reconstruction and PF movement. Linguistic Inquiry 29.569–97.

Baker, C.L. 1970. Problems of polarity in counter-factuals. Studies presented to Robert B. Lees by his Students, ed. by J.M. Sadock and A.L. Vanek, 1–15. Carbondale, IL: Linguistic Research.

Barss, A. 1986. Chains and anaphoric dependence. Cambridge, MA: MIT dissertation.

Barss, A. 2001. Syntactic reconstruction effects. The handbook of contemporary syntactic theory, ed. by M. Baltin and C. Collins, 670–96. Oxford: Blackwell Publishers.

Belletti, A. 1990. Generalized verb movement. Turin, Italy: Rosenberg & Sellier.

Benmamoun, E. 1997. Licensing of negative polarity items in Moroccan Arabic. Natural Language and Linguistic Theory 15.263–87.

Benmamoun, E. 2000. The feature structure of functional categories: a comparative study of Arabic dialects. New York: Oxford University Press.

Bhandari, R. 1998. On the role of tense for negative polarity items licensing. Paper presented at the annual meeting of the Linguistic Society of America, New York.

Bhatia, T.K. 1978. A syntactic and semantic description of negation in South Asian languages. Urbana, IL: University of Illinois at Urbana-Champaign dissertation.

Bhatt, R. 1994. Word order, configurationality and the structure of Kashmiri clause. Theoretical perspective on word order in South Asian languages, ed. by M. Butt, T. King, and G. Ramchand, 31–66. Stanford, CA: CSLI Publications.

Bhatt, R. 1999. Verb movement and the syntax of Kashmiri. Dordrecht, Netherlands: Kluwer Academic Publishers.

Carden, G. 1967. English quantifiers. Cambridge, MA: Harvard University masters dissertation.

Chomsky, N. 1957. Syntactic structures. The Hague: Mouton Publishers.

Chomsky, N. 1981. Lectures on government and binding. Dordrecht, Netherlands: Foris.

Chomsky, N. 1989. Some notes on the economy of derivation and representation, ed. by I. Laka. and A.K. Mahajan, 43–74. MIT working papers in linguistics 10. Cambridge, MA: MITWPL.

Chomsky, N. 1995. The minimalist program. Cambridge, MA: MIT Press.

Cinque, G. (ed.) 1999. Adverbs and functional heads: a cross-linguistics perspective. New York: Oxford University Press.

Comrie, B. 1978. Ergativity. Syntactic typology, ed. by W.P. Lehmann, 329–94. Austin, TX: University of Texas Press.

Dayal, V. 1998. *Any* as inherently modal. Linguistics and Philosophy 21.433–76.

Déprez, V. 1989. On the typology of syntactic positions and the nature of chains. Cambridge, MA: MIT dissertation.

Dixon, R.M.W. 1994. Ergativity. London: Cambridge University Press.

Dwivedi, V. 1991. Negation as a functional projection in Hindi. Proceedings of the western conference on linguistics, ed. by K.Hunt, T. Perry, and V. Samiian [is there an editor?], 88–101. Fresno: California State University Press.

Gaeffke, P. 1968. Untersuchungen zur Syntax des Hindi. The Hague: Mouton and Company.

Gambhir, V. 1981. Syntactic restrictions and discourse functions of word order in standard Hindi. Philadelphia, PA: University of Pennsylvania dissertation.

Guru, K.P. 1952. Hindi vyakaran. Banaras: Nagri Pracharni Sabha.

Haegeman, L. 1995. The syntax of negation. Cambridge, U.K.: Cambridge University Press.

Hook, P.E. 1974. The compound verb in Hindi. Ann Arbor, MI: Center for South and Southeast Asian Study, University of Michigan.

Horn, L.R. 1978. Some aspects of negation. Universals of human language, ed. by J.H. Greenberg, C.A. Ferguson, and E.A. Moravcsik, 127–210. Volume 4. Stanford, CA: Stanford University Press.

Horn, L.R. 1989. A natural history of negation. Chicago, IL: Chicago University Press.

Huang, C-T.J. 1993. Reconstruction and the structure of VP. Linguistic Inquiry 24.103–38.

Jackendoff, R. 1969. An interpretive theory of negation. Foundations of language, 5.2. 218–41.

Kachru, Y. 1965. A transformational treatment of Hindi verbal syntax. London: University of London dissertation.

Kachru, Y. 1966. An introduction to Hindi syntax. Urbana, IL: University of Illinois Press.

Kachru, Y. 1980. Aspects of Hindi grammar. Delhi: Manohar Publications.

Kellogg, S.H. 1938. Grammar of the Hindi language. London: Routledge and Kegan Poul Ltd.

Kidwai, A. 2002. XP adjunction in universal grammar: scrambling and binding in Hindi-Urdu. Oxford: Oxford University Press.

Klima, E. 1964. Negation in English. The structure of language, ed. by J. Fodor and J. Katz, 246–323. Englewood Cliffs, NJ: Prentice-Hall.

Kuroda, S-Y. 1988. Whether we agree or not. A comparative Syntax of English and Japanese. Linguisticae Investigationes 12.1–47.

Ladusaw, W. 1979. Polarity sensitivity as inherent scope relations. Austin, TX: University of Texas at Austin dissertation.

Lahiri, U. 1998. Focus and negative polarity in Hindi. Natural Language Semantics 6.57–123.

Laka, I. 1989. Constraints on sentence negation. Functional heads and clause structure, ed. by I. Laka. and A.K. Mahajan, 199–216. MIT working papers in linguistics 10. Cambridge, MA: MITWPL.

Laka, I. 1994. On the syntax of negation. New York and London: Garland Publishing.

Lakoff, R. 1969. A syntactic argument for negative transportation. CLS 5.140–47.

Lasnik, H. 1972. Analysis of negation in English. Cambridge, MA: MIT dissertation.

Lasnik, H. 1975. On the semantics of negation. Contemporary research in philosophical logic and linguistic semantics, ed. by D.J. Hockney et al., 279–311. Dordrecht, Netherlands: Reidel Publishing.

Lasnik, H. 1981. Restricting the theory of transformations: a case study. Explanations in linguistics: the logical problem in language acquisition, ed. by N. Hornstein and D. Lightfoot, 152–73. London: Longman.

Lasnik, H., and M. Saito. 1992. Move alpha: conditions on its application and output. Cambridge, MA: MIT Press.

Li, Audrey. 1992. Indefinite *wh* in Mandarin Chinese. Journal of East Asian Linguistics 1.125–55.

Linebarger, M.C. 1980. The grammar of negative polarity. Cambridge, MA: MIT dissertation.

Linebarger, M.C. 1987. Negative polarity and grammatical representation. Linguistics and Philosophy 10.325–387.

Mahajan, A.K. 1990a. LF conditions on negative polarity item licensing. Lingua 80.333–48.

Mahajan, A.K. 1990b. The A/A-bar distinction and movement theory. Cambridge, MA: MIT dissertation.

Mahajan, A.K. 1994. Toward a unified theory of scrambling. Studies on scrambling: movement and non-movement approaches to free word-order phenomenon, ed. by N. Corver and Henk van Riemsdijk, 301–330. Berlin and New York: Mouton de Gruyter.

Mohanan, T. 1994. Argument structure in Hindi. Stanford, CA: CSLI Publications.

Pollock, J-Y. 1989. Verb movement, universal grammar, and the structure of IP. Linguistic Inquiry 20.3. 365–424.

Progovac, L. 1988. A binding approach to polarity sensitivity. Los Angeles: University of Southern California dissertation.

Progovac, L. 1994. Negative and positive polarity. Cambridge, U.K.: Cambridge University Press.

Reinhart, T. 1976. The syntactic domain of anaphora. Cambridge, MA: MIT dissertation.

Rizzi, L. 1997. The finite structure of the left periphery. Elements of grammar, ed. by L. Haegeman, 281–337. Dordrecht, Netherlands: Kluwer Academic Publishers.

Shapiro, M.C. 1974. Aspects of Hindi abstract verbal syntax. Chicago, IL: University of Chicago dissertation.

Sportiche, D. 1988. Partitions and atoms of clause structure: subjects, agreement, case, and clitics. London and New York: Routledge.

Srivastav, V. 1994. Binding facts in Hindi and the scrambling phenomenon. Theoretical perspective on word order in South Asian languages, ed. by M. Butt, T. King, and G. Ramchand, 237–61. Stanford, CA: CSLI Publications.

Subbarao, K.V. 1984. Complementation and Hindi syntax. Delhi: Academic Publications.

Travis, L. 1988. The Syntax of Adverbs. Special issue on comparative Germanic syntax, ed. by D. Fekete and Z. Laubitz, 280–310. McGill Working Papers in Linguistics. Montreal: McGill University.

Uribe-Echevarria, M. 1994. Interface licensing conditions on negative polarity items: a theory of polarity and tense interactions. Storrs: University of Connecticut dissertation.

van Olphen, H. 1970. The structure of the Hindi verb phrase. Austin, TX: University of Texas at Austin dissertation.

Vasishth, S. 1997. Neg-criterion and negative polarity licensing in Hindi. Journal of Language and Culture 6.159–76.

Vasishth, S. 1998. Negative contexts and negative polarity in Hindi. The year book of South Asian languages and linguistics, ed. by R. Singh, 135–58. New Delhi: Sage Publications.

Yoon, J.H. 1994. Korean verbal inflection and checking theory. MIT Working Papers in Linguistics 22.251–70.

Zanuttini, R. 1991. Syntactic properties of sentential negation: a comparative study of Romance languages. Philadelphia, PA: University of Pennsylvania dissertation.

Index